THE FLOOR IS LAVA

and 99 more games for everyone, everywhere

IVAN BRETT

GALLERY BOOKS

New York   London   Toronto   Sydney   New Delhi

To my mum, for all of this.

———

G

Gallery Books
An Imprint of Simon & Schuster, Inc.
1230 Avenue of the Americas
New York, NY 10020

Copyright © 2018 by Ivan Brett
Originally published in 2018 in Great Britain by Headline Publishing Group

First Gallery Books trade paperback edition May 2019

GALLERY BOOKS and colophon are registered
trademarks of Simon & Schuster, Inc.

For information about special discounts for bulk purchases,
please contact Simon & Schuster Special Sales at 1-866-506-1949
or business@simonandschuster.com.

The Simon & Schuster Speakers Bureau can bring authors
to your live event. For more information or to book an event,
contact the Simon & Schuster Speakers Bureau at 1-866-248-3049
or visit our website at www.simonspeakers.com.

Manufactured in the United States of America

3   5   7   9   10   8   6   4

Library of Congress Cataloging-in-Publication Data is available.

ISBN 978-1-9821-1618-7
ISBN 978-1-9821-1620-0 (ebook)

CONTENTS

INTRODUCTION

Is This a Game to You?

What is it about playing games? We spend our infancy learning through them, our childhood longing for them, our teenage years accusing people of them, then our adult life pretending they don't exist. Being somebody who plays games—a gamer, I suppose—is either an insult or a badge of honor depending on whom you ask, but it's never just "normal."

I'm going to admit something to you. I spend pretty much all my waking life playing games. I see how many green lights I can go through on my bike by cycling extra slow if I'm approaching a red. I tally my daily writing word count on a complicated spreadsheet and compete against previous weeks, just for the competition. I get to sleep by distracting my mind with a round of **"A–Z of . . ."** (see page 214). I play this thing called "Pokey Sausage" with my cat where we jab each other through the crack in the bathroom door.

The games I play split neatly into two categories: those that make mundane time less mundane, and those that bring people closer together. Playing my life, rather than living it, gives it a sort of structure. It imposes a bunch of unthreatening goals to help me get from point to point. It gives me a way to measure my successes and revel in my daily challenges. Also, playing my life is just more fun than not playing it. And I want to share that with you.

Why Does It Matter?

This book actually started as a manual to teach creative writing. (Don't worry, it isn't anymore!) Then, without my permission, the book shifted form and the games took over. They repainted the walls, chucked out all the pages of grammar, and invited their badly behaved friends. Now the book is bursting with any game that can bring people together, encourage communication, spark creativity, warm you up, cool you down, break an awkward silence, start a party . . .

There's no sacred message to this book. I won't stand behind my lectern and tell you that games are proven to do this or stop that, cure this or shrink that. What I will say is that for me, games provide an opportunity to connect. In an age when so much entertainment and information is available to us at the press of one finger, it's incredibly easy to remain cut off from those immediately around us.

I'm not telling you to get off your phone. I'm not telling you that screens are evil. I am saying there's an alternative. The right game, in the right situation, is better than anything else in the world. I promise, it'll be more fun for both you and your thumb than the scrolling you were about to do, and much less effort than you realize. That's why I wrote this book.

Who Cares?

In researching and compiling this book, I've been fascinated by people's reactions to my elevator pitch. Some seem confused. "Like . . . just games?" they ask. They wonder what purpose the games will serve, or what they will help people achieve, as if the playing of the game isn't enough of an achievement in itself.

Others' eyes light up. "I've got this brilliant game! We played it as kids," they'll say, or "Oh, I loved this one!" I'll bask in their delight as they tell me the rules, noting it down so I don't forget, and wondering why they sound so nostalgic. It's as if these games are off-limits now.

Most people, once they've offered their favorite game, will ask hungrily for mine. The answer is different depending on the weather, or the color of my socks, but I'd probably have to choose between the tactical yet simple **Hangman Mastermind** (see page 82), the bluffs and suspense of **Mafia** (page 104), or the mind-blowingly bonkers experience that is **1,000 Blank White Cards** (page 154). To be honest, my favorite game changes all the time. It'll probably change again before the end of this introduction.

I adore passing games on to a new player. There's a currency in the trading of games—a mischievous delight in simply imagining the fun that could be had. So, here you go. Have a hundred games.

So What's the Point of This Book?

This book is a big green play-button. It's a collection of a hundred creative, comical, cooperative games, grouped together for each situation when you might need them. Going on vacation? There's a chapter for that. Trying to spend more quality time together at dinner? You'll find ten perfect games to play at the table. Stuck inside on a rainy Sunday? Problem solved. Locked in a woefully slow traffic jam? Don't panic. You're good.

The games within this book range from inspiring to challenging to down-right silly, but they're guaranteed to bring you together, liven up any occasion, and even stretch your brain a little. My aim is to turn your life into a game, because we humans do the best sort of learning, connecting, and discovering when we're at play.

All Right, Fine. Where Do I Start?

Absolutely anywhere. I've divided the chapters up into ten different situations that you might find yourself stuck in. Each has ten games perfect for that time. However, there's a lot of crossover, so just dive inside and enjoy yourself. And let me know how you get on! I'm easiest to get hold of on Twitter: @IvanBrett.

CHAPTER 1
TRAFFIC JAMS

Traffic has ground to an absolute halt; there's some sort of accident up ahead. The temporary lights have been red for what feels like a year. There's a dog in the back seat of the car in front, turning anxious circles and barking inaudibly. The kids are ten minutes late for swimming already, and you're not even through the busy part of town. You're cursing yourself for not taking the shortcut around the industrial park. The radio tuner is stuck on smooth classics. What you need is something to take your mind off it.

And that's what I've got for you here. This chapter contains the ten best car games to play when all you've got is each other, a nose-smudged window, and time to waste. These games need no equipment. They're fun enough to distract you from the mind-numbing traffic and will enable you to use the busy streets as a resource. When you actually make it to swimming in time for the last five minutes, you'll feel mildly disappointed, because nothing's as much fun as yelling pirate noises at passing pedestrians or beating your family at **Car Cricket**.

1. Car Cricket

PLAYERS	DIFFICULTY	TIME
2+	Easy	1 hour (at least!)

IN SHORT: Turn traffic into a game with this excellent "cricket" match.

TAGS: MATH, COMPETITIVE, PASS THE TIME

WHAT YOU'LL NEED

- A road with plenty of cars.

- Absolutely no prior knowledge of cricket.

HOW TO PLAY

Test Cricket is one of the oldest and strangest of all British sports. It's a bit like baseball . . . except the game lasts five full days, the pitch is a narrow rectangle rather than a diamond, and all the players must wear white. The two batsmen must protect their wicket (a strange wooden construction made of "stumps" and "bails") from being hit by the ball, while smacking the ball around the field and legging it across to the other end of the pitch, to score runs. Got that? Right. Well, you won't be playing cricket, so don't worry if you didn't. Cricket was a massive part of my childhood, though, so you can imagine why games that used its scoring system were my absolute favorite.

First of all, you'll need a steady stream of cars. Too many, and you'll lose track—too few, and you'll get bored. If you're on a highway, you can use cars that pass (or pass you) on your side. If you're on a quieter road, you can use cars that pass in the other direction.

The game works as follows: each player will take turns to "have a bat."

Just like in cricket, you are aiming to score runs, without getting bowled out. Each time you pass a vehicle, you should add on a different number of runs:

- If you pass a car **(NOT white),** then you score 1 run.

- If you pass a van, caravan, or truck **(again, NOT white),** then you score 2 runs.

- If you pass a motorbike or bicycle, then you score 4 runs.

- If you pass any rare vehicle (such as a horse-drawn carriage, a boat, or a witch on a broom), then you score 6 runs.

- **HOWEVER, if you pass a WHITE CAR, then you are OUT!**

- If you pass any other white vehicle, as long as it isn't a car, then you add no runs for that vehicle, but you are not out. It's a "dot ball." Close one!

Once you are out, note down or remember your score, and the game immediately passes to the next batsman. The game works best if each player has at least two innings, then adds up their total score from each one.

NOW TRY THIS

- If you're a stats nerd, like me, then somebody should have a piece of paper or a device and note down all the scores. Then you can work out batting averages, longest innings, fastest scorers, and all sorts of other things. There's no good reason to do this . . . which is all the better reason to do it!

2. Sail the Seven Seas

PLAYERS	DIFFICULTY	TIME
2+	Easy	The entire car journey

IN SHORT: Turn your journey into a pirate adventure.

TAGS:
PASS THE TIME,
MEMORY, SILLY

WHAT YOU'LL NEED

• Nothing at all.

HOW TO PLAY

Everyone in the car is a bloodthirsty pirate. There are various things throughout your journey that you should keep your one good eye out for:

• If your car stops directly beside another, shout, "Fire the cannons!"

• If you see a pond, lake, ocean, or river, shout, "Sail the seven seas!"

• If you pass a bar, shout, "Ho ho ho and a bottle o' rum!"

• When you see a sign with your destination, shout, "Land, ahoy!"

• Every time you see a car with a broken light, hold your hand over one eye and shout, "Arrr, me eyepatch!"

• Every time you see a bird, shout, "Pretty Polly!"

• Every time somebody crosses the road, shout, "Landlubbers!"

The aim is to be the first person to shout out any of the pirate calls. Remember, it counts only if you do it in your best pirate accent.

NOW TRY THIS

• This game lends itself very well to creativity. When would you shout "Walk the plank?" or "Arrr, treasure!," for example?

3. Where's Voldemort?

PLAYERS	DIFFICULTY	TIME
2+	Easy	The rest of your life

IN SHORT: A background game that'll never get old.
Don't look, or you might get cursed!

TAGS:
LONG-TERM,
COMPETITIVE,
SILLY,
STRATEGY

WHAT YOU'LL NEED

* Nothing at all.

HOW TO PLAY

Thanks to my friend Charlie for inspiration on this one. It's a background game. In other words, it goes on for the entire journey and beyond, whether you know it or not.

The first time you get in the car, explain the rules. After this, as long as everybody knows the rules, you never have to explain them again, or even announce that you're playing.

The rules themselves are simple. Whoever introduces the game starts off as "cursed." To get rid of the curse, simply point out the window and proclaim suddenly, "There's Voldemort!" If you manage to get anybody in your car to look in the direction you've pointed, then they are landed with the curse instead.

If everybody in the car looks, then the person who looks *first* is cursed. Now it's their job to make somebody else look, in order to pass the curse on.

So, the key is to NOT look when somebody else says it, while doing yours in a way that makes people want to see. Obviously, the more often you say the words, the less likely people are to look, so if you're cursed, you've got to save it up until nobody's thinking about it.

Winning this game is all about making your voice and expression so convincing that people don't even realize they're losing the game until they've already lost. One tactic might be to add other words before the dreaded phrase to hide it, or to gasp and point in a *really* believable way. But it's up to you.

TIPS

- Of course, if you use the same sentence ("Look over there! There's Voldemort!") every time, people might get wise to it quite quickly. You could pose a question, pretending to ask about something in the distance, and then drop the V-word once people are looking. Or, how about moderating your tone so that people feel the need to see what you're angry about, or sad about, or amazed by?

- If you actually see Lord Voldemort, it's best not to point. Try running, hiding, or crying. Also, dodging. He has good aim.

4. Destination Sentences

PLAYERS	DIFFICULTY	TIME
2+	**Easy**	**Endless**

IN SHORT: A simple and silly game, turning your destination town or city into sentences.

WHAT YOU'LL NEED

TAGS:
SPELLING,
GRAMMAR,
CREATIVE

- Nothing at all.

HOW TO PLAY

It might feel like you'll never get there with this traffic, but on every car journey you've got a destination in mind. In this game you use that destination to create silly acronyms, and then vote on your favorites. So let's say you're driving to Atlanta. Everybody in the car should try to think of a sentence (or just a phrase) in which the words start with the letter A, then T, then L, and so on. And that's the game! If you like competition, then one player could be the judge and pick a winner and you could give out points. But really, the aim of the game is just to make your sentences either funny or clever.

EXAMPLE

Judge: "Okay, Atlanta. What have you got?"
Player 1: "A terrifying lion attacked nearly thirty antelopes."
Player 2: "Adele took liberties at noodle time. Adele!"
Player 3: "All the little anteaters need ten ants."

NOW TRY THIS

- Of course, once you've done your destination, you could do any place in the world. The longer the word, the harder the round.

- In the UK, we play this with license plates, but that's because there are more letters in ours. So if you're on our side of the pond, why not try it? If a license plate was BR27 ALT, the sentence could be "Ben rode 27 aardvarks last Tuesday."

5. 1-2-3-Spy

PLAYERS	DIFFICULTY	TIME
1+	Easy	Ongoing

IN SHORT: Watch out the window for the numbers
1–999. Spot them, in order, to win.

TAGS:
COLLABORATIVE,
COMPETITIVE,
MATH

WHAT YOU'LL NEED

• Nothing at all.

HOW TO PLAY

This is a sort of I-Spy, or scavenger hunt, where your challenge is to find the
numbers from **1 to 999**, in order, written down in the real world. I've put this
in the Traffic Jams chapter because it's perfect for passing time with your
forehead glued to the window, but there is a drawback: if you're moving, it's
quite easy to pretend you've seen a number and hard for the others to go
back and check. For that reason, if you want to play this competitively, try
it if your car is at a standstill or if you're walking around your local town.

The game works pretty simply: everybody has to look for numbers written
in figures (so 1, not "one") *outside the car*. Any number inside the car doesn't
count, because you could just write it, or look at every page number in this
book. For the same reason, you can't just hold your book out of the window
and flick the pages. Naughty, naughty. Do this properly or don't do it at all.

Players begin by looking for 1. If you're working together, which I recommend, then shout the number out when you see it and share where it was
hiding. You're all now looking for 2. If you're playing against each other, then
the first person to see the 1 gets it, and everybody else has to look for another.
If you shout the number at the same time, you both get it.

Your number can be in the middle of others. So, for example, if you see
"1381," you can use this for **"1"** or **"38"** but definitely not **"31"** or **"11"** because
you're having to cherry-pick from two places.

TIPS

- House numbers, license plates, and roadside ads are great places to find numbers.

- If you think people are just pretending they've seen the numbers, it stops being fun. You could have a rule where two people need to see it, in order to verify that the number was really there. Or just play with people you trust.

NOW TRY THIS

- I set up a round of this game with my other half, Amy, working as a number-spotting team on a shivery night-bus home, and it cheered up our journey to no end. What I didn't predict was that the game ran and ran long after we'd stepped off the bus: we now send each other picture messages containing the next number in the sequence. Until we reach infinity, which may take some time, this game really has no end! Obviously, the same rules still apply: no looking at page numbers, no typing or writing the digits. You have to find them out *in the wild*.

6. I've Just Seen . . .

PLAYERS	DIFFICULTY	TIME
2+	Medium	15 mins

IN SHORT: Describe something out the window, include one lie, and try to get away with it.

WHAT YOU'LL NEED

TAGS:
CONVERSATION,
ON-THE-SPOT,
STRATEGY

- A piece of paper and a pencil, to keep score (not essential).

HOW TO PLAY

We used to play a version of this game with Mr. Perry back when I was a kid. He was formidable at guessing our lies, and we never knew how. Now that I'm all grown up, I realize it's because there are a million ways to spot a liar, and we kids hadn't quite mastered it yet. Nevertheless, I still don't have the skills that Mr. Perry did at rooting out the lie, even though I'm a teacher. Call me too trusting, I guess.

The game works like this: All players close their eyes except the driver (obviously) and one player who'll be the spotter. They must look for something out of the car window. It could be a person, a road sign, an interesting rock, anything. In the few seconds before it's out of sight, the player should try to remember as much as they can about this thing.

Now the rest of the players reopen their eyes and the spotter must describe the item they've memorized, beginning with the phrase "I've just seen . . ." They need to use as much detail as possible, at least five different facts about this item: its size, location, color, what it was made of, what it was doing, and so on. However, the spotter should also include one lie about the item. That lie could be something innocuous, like the fact that the man had a mustache, or something significant, such as the fact that he was flying.

The other players should listen carefully and, at the end of the description, take a guess at which was the lie. Once they've all guessed, the player should reveal the actual lie. If they get it right, they get a point. For every person who doesn't recognize your lie, you get a point.

Once everybody has described something and scored points, the game is over. If you want to extend it, everybody could have another go. By this point you might be getting familiar with what each player does to cover up their lie. For this reason, this game gets better with each repetition!

EXAMPLE

Player 1 (spotter): *"I've just seen a bakery with big wedding cakes in the window. The shop was full of customers, and there was a dog waiting outside. The sign said 'Flour Power,' and the whole shop was pink."*
Player 2: *"I think the shop wasn't pink. Maybe it was white."*
Player 3: *"I don't think it was called Flour Power."*
Player 4: *"I reckon there weren't any wedding cakes in the window."*
Player 1: *"A point to Player 3! It was actually called 'Muffin to Lose.'"*

Player 1 also picks up two points for the other two incorrect guesses, and Player 2 now looks out for his item.

NOW TRY THIS

- When I first played this game, players were allowed to interrupt the description at any time with questions. If asked more about your lie, you'd have to keep on lying to elaborate it. It's up to you whether you allow questions or not. It makes for a very different game, and with many players, it's totally impossible.

7. Cat Eats Mouse

PLAYERS	DIFFICULTY	TIME
2+	Medium	20 mins

IN SHORT: A back-and-forth game of one-upmanship where you must find something to defeat the previous winner.

TAGS: CREATIVE, GRAMMAR, SILLY

WHAT YOU'LL NEED

* Nothing at all.

HOW TO PLAY

This game is a fun mixture of Rock/Paper/Scissors and that old song "I Know an Old Lady Who Swallowed a Fly." Basically, the idea is that everything has a weakness, and that there's always something better if you look hard enough.

One player starts by suggesting a small thing. (I use mouse for my example. Feel free to take that. Otherwise, try beetle, fingernail, metal nail, cube of cheese, penny, Lego piece, worm—anything, really . . .)

The next player must think of something that beats, destroys, uses, outshines, embarrasses, belittles, or generally outdoes the previous thing. They give their answer in the format **"[New thing] [verb] [old thing]."**

The next player must then think of an item that outdoes the most recent item, and so on. You can have a pretty loose idea of what counts as "beating" the previous item, to keep the game going for as long as possible.

You know what? This game is best explained in the example on the next page. (Watch how I use a new verb each time to describe *how* A beats B. You can never just say "Hammer beats nail." It's "Hammer *hits* nail," for example.)

EXAMPLE

Player 1: *"Mouse."*

Player 2: *"Cat eats mouse."*

Player 3: *"Girl strokes cat."*

Player 4: *"Boy chases girl."*

Player 1: *"PlayStation tempts boy."*

Player 2: *"Boot smashes PlayStation."*

Player 3: *"Fire melts boot."*

Player 4: *"Water drenches fire."*

Etc.

TIPS

- It's very tempting to try to "win" this game. I could choose the most powerful thing in the universe and then argue against anybody who tries to beat it. A piece of advice—this game is most fun when someone beats a huge power with something tiny, even if in reality it doesn't make sense. I'm thinking "mouse scares Superman" or "cork plugs black hole." These moments give a great image and provide a giggle. And that's why we're here, isn't it?

- As an extra rule, you could decide that you are never allowed to repeat an object, even in the next round. You'll constantly have to think of new solutions.

8. How Did Liverpool Get Its Name?

PLAYERS	DIFFICULTY	TIME
2+	Medium	30 mins +

IN SHORT: Pick a place on the map and tell the story of how it got its name.

TAGS: CREATIVE, STORYTELLING, CONVERSATION

WHAT YOU'LL NEED

- A map of the surrounding area (alternatively, road signs have plenty of good names on them).

HOW TO PLAY

I made up this game with my dad on the way up to Scotland on our summer vacation. It's such fun, especially if you *really* pretend to know what you're talking about.

Find a town or village nearby on the map, with an interesting name. If you're in the UK, there are thousands of oddly named towns and villages, but even if you're driving through a place where everything nearby has a pretty normal name, that just means you'll have to work your imagination a bit harder.

Now, tell the other players the story of how your place got its name. Try to break the place name down into smaller words, then use your story to build those together into a satisfying conclusion. Check out my example if you need some help. The sillier your story is, the better it is.

EXAMPLE

A Viking hunter called Ulf liked to hunt deer in the local woods. He would bring them home and roast them over his fire, handing out crispy chunks of venison meat to all of his friends and relations. However, the one part of the deer that nobody wanted to eat was the liver.

"Too salty," some would say, or "Too tough!"

Every time, the liver was left over. Afterward, the skin was tanned and made into clothing, the bones ground down to make bonemeal, but the liver remained on the side, hated by all. So Ulf would be forced, each time, to throw the liver into a nearby pond.

Ulf was such a good hunter that even when hundreds of people came to build their Viking huts near his house, around this pond, he was still able to hunt enough deer to keep them all fed. But with more deer came more livers, still uneaten, and thrown into the pond. Eventually the pond was swimming with livers, full to the brim of the stinking slippery things, and it began to be known as the Liver Pool.

So famous was Ulf's Liver Pool that Viking people flocked from far and wide to see it. And that's how Liverpool got its name.

TIPS

- It's quite good fun if every player has a go at describing how the same place got its name. You'll be surprised how different everybody's ideas will be.

- If you're struggling to think of an idea, and breaking the name down doesn't help, remember that over the thousands of years of our history, the spellings and pronunciations of names change hugely, so be quite free with it. For example, Manchester could be broken up into "Mad Jester" or "Munchy Star" or "Man Just Here." Try saying the place name lots of times, really fast, until the edges start to blur.

9. Reg!

PLAYERS	DIFFICULTY	TIME
1+	Hard	**2 mins per license plate**

IN SHORT: Try to "solve" the license plate of the car in front of you. Can you do it before they drive away?

TAGS: MATH, CODE, STRATEGY

WHAT YOU'LL NEED

• A traffic jam, or a busy road where you'll all be able to see the same license plate for longer than a moment.

• Paper and pencil for your workings out, if you need it.

HOW TO PLAY

This game requires some pretty speedy mental math, so be ready for that.

Start by selecting a license plate on a car you can all see. It should have a mixture of letters and numbers (unless you're in Arizona, where you get only numbers). These are going to be your ingredients.

Before anything else, you must convert any letters on the license plate into numbers using the following letter = number code. Pretty soon you'll be able to do this automatically, but to save you some effort, here it is:

A = 1	E = 5	I = 9	M = 13	Q = 17	U = 21	Y = 25
B = 2	F = 6	J = 10	N = 14	R = 18	V = 22	Z = 26
C = 3	G = 7	K = 11	O = 15	S = 19	W = 23	
D = 4	H = 8	L = 12	P = 16	T = 20	X = 24	

So in the license plate TJU9134, we have T = 20, J = 10, U = 21, and then 9, 1, 3, and 4. If you have the number 0, treat it as the letter O (which is 15).

Your job is to add, subtract, multiply, and divide these numbers to reach your target of 100. You can use each number only once, but you don't have to use them all. (Not every license plate works, but most do, so don't give up!)

In this case, you can do 4 + 1 = 5, then multiply by T (20) to make 100.

If you solve the license plate, shout "REG!" Explain the solution to the other players to finish the round.

TIPS

- If these calculations take too long and cars never stay still for long enough, you'll need to write them down. Never photograph anybody's license plate without permission. They won't like it.

- If you're finding this all too difficult, then it might help to use this slightly simplified letter = number code. It uses only numbers up to ten.

A, K, U = 1	F, P, Z = 6
B, L, V = 2	G, Q = 7
C, M, W = 3	H, R = 8
D, N, X = 4	I, S = 9
E, O, Y = 5	J, T = 10

10. I'm in Business

PLAYERS	DIFFICULTY	TIME
2+	**Hard**	**Ongoing**

IN SHORT: Puns about jobs, in a silly conversation game.

TAGS: PUNS, COLLABORATIVE, CONVERSATION

WHAT YOU'LL NEED

• Nothing at all.

HOW TO PLAY

This is the sort of game to introduce at the start of a journey and just let brew. You might blurt out a suggestion, then leave it again until you pass Birmingham. It's hard, and good ideas take time. Everyone's a winner here, so just have a go and enjoy it.

So, the game always works with the same five lines of conversation.

    1: "I'm in business."
    2: "Oh yeah? What's your business?"
    1: "I'm a _____."
    2: "How's it going?"
    1: " _____."

Each time, Player 1 has to give a job, and then provide a pun about how that job's going.

. . . And that's it! It's great because you can go on forever. There are a million jobs, and for each one, many ways to create a pun about it. Here are a couple of examples:

EXAMPLE

Player 1: *"I'm in business."*
Player 2: *"Oh yeah? What's your business?"*

Player 1: *"I'm an engraver."*
Player 2: *"How's it going?"*
Player 1: *"I scratch a living."*

Player 3: *"I'm in business."*
Player 4: *"Oh yeah? What's your business?"*
Player 3: *"I'm a bungee-jumping instructor."*
Player 4: *"How's it going?"*
Player 3: *"It has its ups and downs."*

(I won't punish you with any more. Now it's up to you!)

TIP

- When you're thinking about your next submission, it's actually easier to start with the comment about how it's going and work backward to the job. If I say, "It's very tiring," then I might make my job something to do with wheels, perhaps . . .

NOW TRY THIS

- This game is essentially just a joke factory. If you're good at these ones, why not try making your own knock-knock jokes? These are similar, in that the person on the other end only has to respond with the same line each time, and the hard work's all yours.

- That reminds me of one of my favorite pranks of all time. Tell your friend that you've got this really good knock-knock joke, then ask them to start. You'll ask "Who's there?" and they'll be stuck having to say the all-important third line without any preparation.

CHAPTER 2
THE KITCHEN TABLE

It's Thursday evening, about half past six. You've done fish fingers, but they burned under the grill because Trish called to ask for advice about her son, who's got worms. Max doesn't even want to come down because he's got his war poets essay due tomorrow, and Clara's refusing to eat anything now that the peas have touched the ketchup. Only a month ago, you enforced the "No TV at the table" rule, but it's slipped again, and for the last couple of weeks your munching has been drowned out by *EastEnders*.

It's time for a change. Here are ten games you could play across the dinner table, whether you're waiting for the juices on that roast to run clear, or chewing your way through an endless plate of vegetables. They require nothing more than the table you're sitting at, and spark off great situations to make the most of the time you spend together.

11. Crambo

PLAYERS	DIFFICULTY	TIME
2+	Medium	10–20 mins

IN SHORT: Guess a secret word with rhymes and synonyms. The whole game creates its own rhyming poem every time. Neat!

TAGS: GRAMMAR, VOCABULARY, RHYME

WHAT YOU'LL NEED

* Nothing at all.

HOW TO PLAY

This is a classic. Dating back to the Middle Ages, **Crambo** is a simple guessing game that works in rhyme.

One player, the rhymer, picks a word. Start with shorter words (one syllable); you can move on to something more complicated once you're all used to the game.

Let's say the rhymer has chosen the word "bed." She will think of a word that rhymes with "bed" and begin the game like this: *"I know a word that rhymes with dead."*

Now the guessers know that they're searching for a word that rhymes with "dead." But they can't just guess. They have to only hint at the word they're guessing.

For example, one guesser thinks of "red." So he asks, *"Is it a color?"*

To which the rhymer would respond, *"No, it's not red."*

Another guesser might ask, *"Is it on top of my neck?"*

To which the rhymer would respond, *"No, not in my head."*

The game continues until a guesser gives a clue that clearly leads to the correct word. The rhymer will respond, *"Yes, it is bed!"*

I've just given an example, but here's another.

EXAMPLE

Rhymer: "I know a word that rhymes with plate."

Guesser 1:   "Is it a garden door?"

Rhymer: "No, not a gate."

Guesser 2:   "Is it disliking?"

Rhymer: "No, it's not hate."

Guesser 3:   "Is it a summer party?"

Rhymer: "No, not a fete."

Guesser 1:   "Is it just brilliant?"

Rhymer: "No, it's not great."

Guesser 2:   "Is it behind time?"

Rhymer: "Yes! It is late!"

TIPS

● This game is so excellent because everybody's doing something. Normally, the person who isn't doing the guessing is just saying yes or no to all the questions chucked at them. In this game, they have to think of the rhyming word each time. For a group where everybody needs to feel involved all of the time, this will work well.

● If the rhymer can't work out the word that you're guessing, keep giving clues, or give the first letter. Never just tell them the word you're guessing.

NOW TRY THIS

● The "question, rhyming answer, question, rhyming answer" format is pretty simple, but why not try to make the whole thing have a rhythm, too? Notice how the rhymer changed the wording of her answers so that they always fit with the meter of the game. If you're really into the rap element, you could beat along with a wooden spoon on the back of a saucepan.

● If you have a particularly great round, why not write it down? Crambo poems are fun, silly, and make the reader guess along with the game. It's rare to find a game that's so much fun to read back over afterward.

12. Kim's Game

PLAYERS	DIFFICULTY	TIME
2+	Easy	2 mins per item

IN SHORT: Hide an item beneath the table. What's missing?

WHAT YOU'LL NEED

TAGS:
MEMORY,
AROUND THE
HOUSE

- A big table full of cutlery, crockery, condiments, and so on. The fuller the better.

HOW TO PLAY

This game involves removing items from the table and potentially hiding them on your lap, so play it before dinner when the plates aren't greasy.

One player, the guesser, closes her eyes. Then, the other players **remove one thing** from the table and hide it underneath. Any of the other players can hide the item, but you can only hide one thing, and it must be a group decision. Nothing else on the table should be moved.

Now the guesser opens her eyes. She may not get up from her chair or look beneath the table. She just needs to look at the table and work out what's missing. Don't block her view of anything on the table!

The guesser only gets **three guesses**. If she gets the item right, make a big deal of revealing the item theatrically. Even if she doesn't, the third guess can be quite a dramatic moment with a big reveal. Enjoy it!

NOW TRY THIS

- This game gets easier with time. Eventually, you'll know the contents of your table pretty well. After a few rounds, limit the player to one guess, or only ten seconds to guess. The other players could even quietly count down, to raise the tension.

13. Please Pass the . . .

PLAYERS	DIFFICULTY	TIME
2+	Easy	20 mins

IN SHORT: That moment when you want to say something, but don't know what it's called, as a game.

TAGS:
PASS THE TIME,
MEMORY, SILLY

WHAT YOU'LL NEED

- A table full of stuff. Dinner tables are perfect.

HOW TO PLAY

This game has two phases. Start with the first and move on to the second. (You can also follow the natural progression of how my family makes up a game by watching how this one develops.) I won't put level 2 in the **Now Try This** section because it's the main game, really. Think of level 1 as an introduction.

LEVEL 1

One player, the mimer, chooses something on the table that she wants. It could be the salt or ketchup, or something the other players would usually pass, but it doesn't need to be. It could be the lid of the mayonnaise jar, or someone else's fork.

Next, the mimer says, "Please pass the . . ." and acts out the thing she wants using only mime. From this point, she cannot say a single word until the correct thing has been passed. Even "No!" should be replaced by a shake of her head. She may absolutely *never* point to the item on the table, and even staring at the item should be discouraged. That would make the game far too easy.

The other players will try to pass her things in the following form: "Here's the salt shaker," "Here's the gravy," "Here's the bottle of poison," but the mimer will refuse everything except the one item she wants. Once the mimer has been passed the correct thing, the game continues when another player will ask for something to be passed.

LEVEL 2

If you're ready to move on, then begin to choose things that aren't on the table. For example, one mimer might choose a dog collar and say, "Please pass the . . ." and then mime putting the collar on a dog. In response, the other players will try to hand her the correct thing, also in mime. They will accompany this with the words "Here's the necklace," "Here's the dog," "Here's the dog collar." The mimer will only accept the third offer, obviously.

TIPS

- Miming is an art. There isn't a correct way to do it, but try not to mouth the words, spell with your fingers, write anything down, or use other "cheating" tactics. You may as well just ask for the thing to be passed, and that isn't a game. That's just dinner.

- Look at all the different ways you can mime an item: you can mime the shape of something, the weight of it, your attitude toward it, what you do with it, and even where you'd find it. For example, if I were miming a vase of flowers, I could pick the flowers, sniff them, slot them into the (heavy) vase, carry the vase to a tap, fill up the water, place on a table, and arrange the flowers carefully. There's so much you can do if the other players aren't imagining what you're imagining.

14. Shut Your Eyes

PLAYERS	DIFFICULTY	TIME
2+	Easy	10 mins +

IN SHORT: You'll never see the contents of a room quite the same after playing this simple memory game.

TAGS: MEMORY, GUESSING

WHAT YOU'LL NEED

- Nothing at all.

HOW TO PLAY

This game changes as you play it, because the more rounds you do, the more aware people become of their surroundings.

It works pretty simply. You don't need to agree to play this game, like most of the others in this book. One player, the questioner, unannounced, tells another, the recaller, to shut their eyes. The questioner then asks the recaller a simple question about the room. For example:

- "What's on the work surface behind you?"

- "How many forks are on the table?"

- "What color is my necklace?"

- "How many people are in the painting on the wall by the door?"

- "How many potatoes are left on your plate?" (This question is best if you have been eating potatoes, but not limited to those occasions. I always keep a spare potato in my pocket to surprise other players when they open their eyes.)

Obviously, the challenge is for the recaller to remember correctly with their eyes firmly closed.

Once the recaller has given their answer, they'll inevitably open their eyes and check, and from this point on, the whole table will be much more aware of everything around them. From question two onward, you can usually make the questions much harder.

15. Boink!

PLAYERS	DIFFICULTY	TIME
2+	Medium	20 mins

IN SHORT: Replace two homophones in a sentence with "BOINK!" for a fun word-guessing game.

TAGS: GRAMMAR, VOCABULARY, SILLY

WHAT YOU'LL NEED

- Access to the Internet for a bigger list of homophones, but only if you get stuck!

HOW TO PLAY

Homophones are two words that are spelled differently, mean different things, but sound the same. So, for instance, "I" and "eye," or "heard" and "herd."

You can put two homophones in the same sentence, with a nice effect:

- "Can you see if **I** have some grit in my **eye**?"

- "The **herd** of cows **heard** the storm approaching."

However, this game requires you *not* to say the homophones. Rather, replace them both with the word "**BOINK**!"

- "Can you see if **BOINK** have some grit in my **BOINK**?"

- "The **BOINK** of cows **BOINK** the storm approaching."

The other players should guess the homophones that "BOINK" has replaced. Of course, the second sentence is easier to guess (and more fun) than the first, because it gives away a few more clues, and there's more to go on.

EXAMPLE

I won't give you too many examples, or I'll spoil the game. But here is a short list of homophones you could use. (In the English language there are hundreds. Part of the game is thinking of them!)

- *to/too/two*
- *where/wear*
- *witch/which*
- *road/rode*
- *wait/weight*

And how about half-homophones, such as close/clothes?

TIPS

- If you're struggling to think of homophones, look online for a few more. The only problem with giving you loads here is that if everyone's already seen them, they're pretty easy to guess.

- Try to fill your sentences with more clues by surrounding the BOINKs with related words. "BOINK! I'm BOINK!" could be anything. Try "BOINK there, fine sir. I'm very BOINK in this tree and need help getting down." In this case, the answer is "hi" and "high."

NOW TRY THIS

- If you're bored of homophones, how about homonyms? These are words that are spelled exactly the same but still mean different things, such as "rose": e.g., "I rose from my armchair" or "No rose could smell so sweet." Homonyms are harder to find, which makes finding them all the more satisfying.

16. King Henry VIII's Banquet

PLAYERS	DIFFICULTY	TIME
2+	Medium	15 mins

IN SHORT: Remember a list of foods that grows and grows.

TAGS:
MEMORY,
CREATIVITY,
SILLY

WHAT YOU'LL NEED

• Nothing at all.

HOW TO PLAY

King Henry VIII was known for his enormous appetite and even larger stomach, so much so that his feasts became legendary. The food he served was gluttonous, extravagant, and often very weird. Roasted swan, grilled beavers' tails, cow's udders, dolphin, all sorts of things. Your goal is to imagine this feast.

This is a great game to play during a mega-meal of your own. Simply, you'll take turns adding a dish of food to King Henry's banquet table, while at the same time remembering all the items that have come before. It's a huge amount of fun, and becomes a real challenge as it progresses.

One player begins with the statement "At his banquet, King Henry ate . . ." and then adds one type of food. It can be as simple or as descriptive as you like, but the general rule is: make it sound expensive or calorific, or just weird.

Now the next player recites the same statement, plus the previous foodstuff (including descriptions), and then adds one of their own. Each subsequent player then continues in the same fashion.

When a player cannot remember one of the items, you could help them by miming it, or giving a little prompt. If they really can't remember, you could finish the game there. Alternatively, if there are at least four of you playing, "buzz out" that player. The next player would now have to recite the whole list and add a new item. See who can stay in the game the longest.

EXAMPLE

Player 1: "At his banquet, King Henry ate a boiled prawn head."

Player 2: "At his banquet, King Henry ate a boiled prawn head and a quadruple cheeseburger."

Player 3: "At his banquet, King Henry ate a boiled prawn head, a quadruple cheeseburger, and a twenty-dollar-bill salad."

Player 4: "At his banquet, King Henry ate a boiled prawn head, a quadruple cheeseburger, and a castle made of toffee."

Player 3: "You forgot the twenty-dollar-bill salad!"

Player 4: "All right, I'm out."

Player 2: "At his banquet . . ."

Etc.

TIPS

- Don't worry about the weird and wonderful foods if you feel pressure to make up amazing ones. Any food is good food.

- Memory is a skill you can learn. Believe me, I have a *terrible* memory, but I'm actually not bad at this game. Some people try to visualize each item in the list. Personally, I like to take it a little further and build a narrative in my head where one item *interacts* with the next, so that all your ideas are connected in a string. So, for example, I'd imagine the boiled prawn head leaking its fishy water and getting the quadruple cheeseburger's bun all soggy. Then the burger is too tall, so it topples onto a plate of sliced twenty-dollar bills. That sort of thing.

17. Six Degrees of Separation

PLAYERS	DIFFICULTY	TIME
1+	Medium	20 mins

IN SHORT: Link two random items in as few steps as possible.

WHAT YOU'LL NEED

TAGS:
CREATIVE,
WIND-DOWN,
PASS THE TIME

- Nothing at all.

HOW TO PLAY

One player picks two random items. If you need some help here, turn to the list of story objects (see pages 237–39) and waggle your finger about with your eyes closed until you land on a word.

It is every player's job to find a string of items that link those two things, in as few steps as possible.

When you're all ready, each player should share their chain of links. If you aren't happy with one of the other player's links, if it's too tenuous, too general, or just plain wrong, challenge the other player on it.

Once you've finished, players should judge whose chain was best by whose was shortest, plus a special prize for the person who may not have got there quickest, yet each link was solid, imaginative, and interesting.

EXAMPLE

Player 1 chose the items this time. She chose SAUSAGE and IVORY.
Player 1: *"You make sausage from a pig, pigs are an animal, one animal is an elephant, ivory comes from elephants. Four steps!"*
Player 2: *"I eat sausages on a plate. Plates are white, and ivory is white."*
(This is three steps, but in my opinion it's not a good answer, as plates can be any color.)
Player 3: *"You pick up sausages with a fork, forks are pointy, tusks are pointy, ivory is made from tusks. Four steps."*

Who won? You decide.

NOW TRY THIS

- It's also quite good fun to play the same game, but with **as many** links as possible. See how long you can keep your chain going before finally falling asleep or reaching your other item.

- You may know of the game "Six Degrees of Kevin Bacon." It's basically the same idea, but you are allowed to use only actors, and your target is always Kevin Bacon. You need to find a film that your actor has starred in, as well as Kevin Bacon. If you can't, then you'll need to go via another actor. So, for example, if you chose Daniel Radcliffe, you would say that Daniel was in *Harry Potter and the Sorcerer's Stone* with John Cleese, and then John Cleese was in *The Big Picture* with Kevin Bacon. Yeah, I had to search online for it. I'm terrible at this game.

18. What's My Line?

PLAYERS	DIFFICULTY	TIME
2+	Medium	10 mins per round

IN SHORT: Guess a player's made-up job.

WHAT YOU'LL NEED

● Nothing at all.

HOW TO PLAY

This is a classic game to play before or during your meal to keep the conversation flowing.

One player, the professional, picks a job and pretends that they do it. You could start off simple (police officer, dairy farmer) but eventually get really niche (newspaper columnist, skydiving instructor). If you get stuck, have a look on pages 231–33 for some inspiration. Plenty of jobs written there.

The questioners take turns asking about the professional's life. Question by question, they should be closing in on the nature of the work.

The professional can answer only yes or no. If the answer is iffy, you could say "Sort of" or "Sometimes," but try to avoid this. If you don't know the answer, say so, but if you find yourself not knowing the answer to lots of questions, you've picked the wrong job.

Once one of the questioners has guessed the job, they can pick one and the game continues.

EXAMPLE

The professional has chosen "prime minister."
Questioner 1: *"Do you have to wear a uniform?"*
Professional: *"No."*
Questioner 2: *"Do you work in an office?"*
Professional: *"Sometimes."*

Questioner 3: *"Do you sell things?"*
Professional: *"No."*
Questioner 1: *"Do you make a lot of money?"*
Professional: *"I don't know. Probably, yes."*
Questioner 2: *"Do I regularly see people who do your job on TV?"*
Professional: *"Yes."*
Etc.

TIP

- This game is so much easier if the job you choose is nice and active. If you choose a certified public accountant or a divorce lawyer, the questioners will need to be very inventive (and possibly quite technical!) to get to the bottom of what it is you actually do.

19. Scat Memory

PLAYERS	DIFFICULTY	TIME
2+	**Hard**	**15 mins**

IN SHORT: Remember, and add to, an increasingly complicated line of "scat" singing.

TAGS: MEMORY, CREATIVE, RHYTHM, SILLY

WHAT YOU'LL NEED

- A kitchen/restaurant/café containing people who don't mind you making some incredibly silly noises.

HOW TO PLAY

This is a tremendous game to play around a table, but don't do it with your mouth full!

If you haven't heard of scat, you're in for a treat. It's a type of rhythmic singing without words, mostly in jazz, where you just make noises along with the music. It's free and improvisational, and there are no rules. You just make the sounds you feel like making.

If you want some excellent examples, search these out online:

- "One Note Samba" by Ella Fitzgerald
- "Heebie Jeebies" by Louis Armstrong
- "Scatman (Ski-ba-bop-ba-dop-bop)" by Scatman John

Okay, so we'll never be as good as them, but we're going to employ the same idea in our game.

Scat singing basically has no limit, but there are some scat "words" you'll have heard coming back quite a few times. They're often plosive, which means they have a "pop" noise. They sometimes imitate percussion noise.

Have a go at saying some of these out loud. Try them forward, backward, fast, and slow:

- Bop
- Bap
- Pah
- Shoop
- Shap
- Skip
- Skee
- Dap
- Diddlee
- Doo
- Woo
- Dee

Feel ready? Okay. One player begins by saying one scat word.

The next player then repeats that scat word and adds another.

Each player repeats all of the scat words and then adds one more word at the end.

Bit by bit, the players will build a scat melody and rhythm. The challenge is to remember what's come before and add something new. The game ends when there are so many "wah"s and "shoop"s in your head that you scat all over the carpet.

EXAMPLE

Player 1: "Boop."
Player 2: "Boop dada."
Player 3: "Boop dada skip."
Player 1: "Boop dada skip bop."
Player 2: "Boop dada skip bop wheep."
Player 3: "Boop skip bop wheep."

But Player 3 forgot "dada." How could she? The players either correct her and carry on, or stop and start a new scat melody.

TIPS

- Really try to work with the rhythm of your scat sequence. "Bap boo shap scap skip dap woo" is all right, but you won't get yourself a Grammy anytime soon. It's too ploddy! Get your feet tapping, put on your darkest jazz sunglasses, and get in the groove with words that build an interesting rhythm.

- While there is no limit to what constitutes a scat "word," try not to add anything too complicated. For example: which is the odd one out in the following scat melody? "Bop dap ba-boop whop, skeedily encyclopedia shoo wap."

• Actually, that last one was kind of catchy.

NOW TRY THIS

• This is such a wonderfully musical game. Stick on some old-fashioned jazz with no singing and play your game over a musical backing track. You'll love the way the melodies grow and fit with the song, and players are forced to impersonate each other to make sense of the words.

20. Hardest Game in the World

PLAYERS	DIFFICULTY	TIME
4+	Hard	Infinite

IN SHORT: How hard can it be to count to twenty?

TAGS: COLLABORATIVE, STRATEGY

WHAT YOU'LL NEED

- Nothing at all.

HOW TO PLAY

I love this game, simply because of what it says about you, the player, based on how you play it. (Quick note: the more players you have for this game, the better.)

The challenge is simple: **count to twenty.**

The twist, however, is in the following rules:

1. You are not allowed to say more than one number at a time.

2. You may not make any motion, sound, or indication to the other players about who should speak next.

3. If two people say the next number simultaneously, it's game over. You must start back at number one.

This is a game of body language. You want someone in the circle to say the next number, but you don't want two people to say it. Deciding on some order or tactic is *strictly* forbidden. Any group can count to twenty if you know who will say each number. This is about communication through other means. What can you see in someone's breathing, their eyes, the way they open their mouth or sit forward?

You must self-police. It's pretty easy to let someone take control or develop some way of showing who's speaking next. Don't let that happen.

NOW TRY THIS

- Obviously, if you find it simple to get to twenty, then try going further. Set a high score and try to beat it with a different group.

- The more players you have, the harder it gets. I've done this with a class of children and never got past eight.

- If you're really attuned to each other, try this game *with your eyes closed*. You'll hate each other, yourselves, and also me for suggesting it, within ten minutes, but it's an excellent challenge.

CHAPTER 3

LONG, HOT SUMMER

Two weeks in sunny Mallorca sounded like an excellent idea in January, but now that you're here, it's hardly the paradise you'd imagined. There are flies in the hotel bathroom, and if you venture outside, you'll be assaulted by the sort of sun that cooks you to crispy bacon in five minutes. Dad's earned himself a squirming tummy from that dodgy paella, the kids don't want to read their vacation books, and their eyes are stinging from a pool that's more chlorine than water. But never fear, because I've got ten games that will let you pass the time smoothly under a shady palm tree. They're slow, creative, and all the better for being left out in the sun to ferment for a while.

In this chapter you'll find secret languages, storytelling games, and a massive murder mystery that will absolutely overtake your vacation. Even if you're at home, there are games here that make that long summer break pass like an August cloud.

21. Twenty-One Dares

PLAYERS	DIFFICULTY	TIME
2+	Easy	15 mins +

IN SHORT: A simple, tactical counting game. You can use it as a springboard to give out dares or forfeits.

TAGS: MATH, STRATEGY, COMPETITIVE

WHAT YOU'LL NEED

• Nothing at all.

HOW TO PLAY

This game can be played anywhere: airport departure lounges, on the beach, or halfway up a mountain. The aim of the game is to avoid saying "twenty-one."

Players take turns counting in order, starting from one, choosing whether to say one number, two, or three. You may not say more than three numbers, and you may not skip, repeat, or go down.

Eventually, one player will be forced to say "twenty-one." They lose, and must be punished! Some sort of dare or forfeit that does not disturb other people would be perfect. If you're in a place where dares aren't appropriate, "truth" questions would be just as good. Ask the loser a question that they *must* answer honestly.

EXAMPLE

Player 1: "One, two, three."
Player 2: "Four, five."
Player 3: "Six, seven, eight."
Player 4: "Nine."
Player 1: "Ten, eleven, twelve."
Player 2: "Thirteen, fourteen."
Player 3: "Fifteen, sixteen, seventeen."

Player 4: *"Eighteen, nineteen."*
Player 1: *"Twenty!"*
Player 2: *"Twenty-one. Darn it."*

Player 2 earns the next dare.

TIPS

- I'm not going to spoil the game here, but it's worth saying that it has been "solved." That is, there is a simple mathematical way to make sure that you never lose, at least when playing with two people. Challenge me, if you meet me; I swear you won't beat me. (I realize that rhymed.)

- This does get more complicated with more players, but there still could be a way to solve it so that you always win. Experiment!

NOW TRY THIS

- If one or more of the players in your group knows how to never lose at this game (see above), you might need another challenge. Try one of these:

- Change the number of numbers that you are allowed to say each turn. The game is vastly different if you're able to count four at a time, or even five.

- Change the target from 21 to 22, or 36, or 81. See how your tactics change.

22. Murder in Paradise

PLAYERS	DIFFICULTY	TIME
4+	Easy	1 day–2 weeks

IN SHORT: Set up this Clue-style "murder" game at the beginning of a vacation, then plan and "execute" your murder when the time is right.

TAGS:
ACTIVE,
LONG-TERM,
STRATEGY

WHAT YOU'LL NEED

- Pens and scraps of paper.

- Three hats, or bowls, or something to pick a slip of paper from.

HOW TO PLAY

If you're about to head off on a big family vacation, then this might be the game to spice up your trip. It's a game of secrets, subterfuge, deception, and, most important, murder. It ought to be said at this point, please don't actually murder anybody. Not even a little bit. You're better than that. Having said that, pretending's fine!

So, you've arrived at your destination and you're lucky enough to be rattling around for two weeks in a beautiful hotel, villa, village, etc. On the first evening, once you've got a feel of the place and know where you can go, what you can do, and so on, sit all the players down and set up the game. It works like this:

1. Write **everybody's name** on slips of paper, fold them up, and put them in **the first hat**. It's really important that every player has their name on a piece of paper just once. Think of a secret Santa.

2. Now, each player should write **a location** within the area where you're staying that you could easily get to. So, it could be "the bakery next door," "Mom and Dad's bedroom," or "under the big tree in the garden," but not "the clouds." Everyone should fold up their sugges-

tion and put it in **the second hat**. Players should not show anyone else what they've written.

3. Finally, every player should write **an object** that is safe and easily accessible. Choose something like "a baguette," "a pillow," or "Amy's sock." Please do not choose anything that could actually be used as a weapon—for example, nothing sharp. Everyone should fold up their suggestion and put it in **the third hat**. Again, the suggestions should be kept secret.

Once this stage is complete, everybody should take turns picking a name from the hat. (If you get yourself, please immediately say so, put it back, and draw again. If the last person gets themselves, you'll need to put all the names back and draw again.) This name is your potential "victim."

Next, pick out a location and an item. These are the requirements for your murder. You now have a victim, a scene of the crime, and a weapon. **Keep them secret**—if anybody finds out, your game will become MUCH harder!

The rest of the vacation is your time limit. All you have to do is get your victim alone in the location on your paper and have the murder weapon with you. Show them your slips of paper, and they're dead!

At this point, you need to tell the other players who killed whom, with what, and where. Not only can you enjoy the silliness of it, but it might help the other potential victims work out who wants them dead.

Meanwhile, you're trying your best to avoid being killed by whoever picked out your name. Bargain, barter, and bluff your way around other players to find out what they know. Keep your eyes peeled for family members carrying around a lemon all the time, or continually asking you to come to the laundry room. These clues might give away a lot!

If you've committed your murder, you must still watch out for the person who's going for you. The game ends only when everybody's either committed their murder or they're dead.

If you're killed, you can't commit your murder anymore, but that doesn't mean you can't play. It's still fun to try to work out who's left, and what their murder plan might be. For that reason, **even if you're dead, don't give away whom you were supposed to kill**. It's much more fun to keep everybody paranoid right until the end.

TIPS

- This game is as much about gathering clues as killing people. If there are four players and you think you know who two others are killing, you've identified your potential murderer. Avoid being alone with them at all costs!

- Keep your slips of paper safe. There's no rule against ferreting out other people's information.

- What's great about this game is that you can freely trade knowledge and insight. For example, if you've spotted your dad carrying around that lemon, you might suspect that's his murder weapon. You could offer that information to your brother in exchange for something he's noticed. If he tells you that Mom's been repeatedly asking *him* to take a look at something in the laundry room, you can probably stop worrying about Mom killing *you* anytime soon.

- At the start, when you open up your location and murder-weapon papers, speak out if you don't think it's fair, or don't think it's within the spirit of the game. If you're being asked to heft your dad and a living whale into the top shelf of the oven, then you won't have a good time.

NOW TRY THIS

- If your vacation involves a lot of moving around, then you might need to pick some more general locations and items. For example, "bedroom" or "restaurant." You could still play the game, as long as you travel to a place that has that thing.

23. Preposition I-Spy

PLAYERS	DIFFICULTY	TIME
2+	Easy	5 mins per round

IN SHORT: Practice prepositions with a fun twist on an old game.

TAGS:
GRAMMAR,
GUESSING,
VOCABULARY

WHAT YOU'LL NEED

• Nothing at all.

HOW TO PLAY

I assume you know how to play the great vacation game I-Spy: "I spy, with my little eye, something beginning with P." "Pizza!"

Well, this isn't that. In this game, you don't give letters but locations. First of all, you need to know about **prepositions**.

Prepositions are little words that are used to give the position of a noun. Pre-*position*. See? So, for example, "The dog hides **under** the carpet," or "We ate our dinner **after** the race." Here are a few more prepositions:

• Inside/outside

• Above/below

• Next to/to the left of/to the right of

• In front of/behind

• Between

Now one player picks an object around her. However well the original I-Spy works in a car, you might need to be moving a little slower than that for this variation.

The player gives her first clue. "I spy, with my little eye, something **below** something beginning with P."

So the other players—the guessers—not only have to look for something beginning with P, but also find an object below it. They each get one guess at the object, not the thing beginning with P, before the first player gives another clue to the same object, using a different preposition. "I spy, with my little eye, something **in front of** something beginning with L."

Once somebody's guessed the object, it's time to swap roles.

EXAMPLE

Player 1: *"I spy, with my little eye, something on something beginning with T."*

Player 2 thinks the T might be that palm tree. "A coconut?"

Player 1: *"Nope."*

Player 3 thinks the T might be a truck driving by. "A roof?"

Player 1: *"Nuh-uh."*

Player 4 thinks the T might be the table. "Your gin and tonic?"

Player 1: *"Wrong. I spy, with my little eye, something behind something beginning with G."*

Player 4 sees that behind the gin and tonic, on the table, is the sunscreen. "Sunscreen?"

Player 1: *"Yep!"*

Player 4 is the winner and picks a new item.

24. Don't Finish the Word!

PLAYERS	DIFFICULTY	TIME
2+	Easy	10–20 mins

IN SHORT: Fun, competitive, and weirdly addictive spelling game.

TAGS:
SPELLING,
STRATEGY,
VOCABULARY,
COMPETITIVE

WHAT YOU'LL NEED

- Pencil and paper/whiteboard (optional). See **NOW TRY THIS**.

HOW TO PLAY

Perfect for playing with your eyes closed, lounging on a hammock, this game will keep you entertained for as long as you need it to. The aim is to add a letter to a word **without finishing it**. Players will take turns saying a letter, adding to the previous letters, and working toward spelling a word (the words in mind will change and evolve as the game progresses). This goes on until somebody finishes a word. If you finish a word, you lose a life.

Sometimes you may suspect that your opponent is just bluffing and they do not have a real word in mind after they've added their letter. At this point, you may declare "Challenge!" Then your opponent has to say the word they were thinking of. If there's an incorrect spelling in the letters you currently have, or if there's no word at all, then they lose a life. If, however, they were working toward a valid word, then you lose a life.

All players begin with five lives. The last player with lives remaining is the winner!

EXAMPLE

First round. **Player 1** *writes* **"T."**
Player 2 *thinks of the word "THE" and writes* **"H."**
Player 1 *cannot write "E" because it would finish the word "THE."*
He writes **"I."**

Player 2 *cannot write "S" because it would finish the word "THIS." She writes* **"N,"** *thinking of the word "THING."*

Player 2 loses a life*, because* **THIN** *is a completed word.*

Second round. **Player 2** *writes* **"G."**

Player 1 *writes* **"L."**

Player 2 *writes* **"U."**

Player 1 *could write "E," "G," or "M," but those letters all finish words. He doesn't think of "C" for "GLUCOSE." Instead, he tries to bluff his opponent. He adds* **"N"** *and hopes she will think he's found a word.*

Player 2 *looks at* **"GLUN"** *for a long time, but eventually declares "Challenge!"*

Player 1 *cannot finish the word.* **Player 1 loses a life.**

TIPS

- Make sure you don't begin with the letters A or I, unless you really like losing lives. Those words are already finished!

- If the only letters you can think of finish the word, try to bluff. Add a random letter and leave it for your opponent to squirm. You'd be surprised how often they do the same in return, and then you can definitely challenge.

- This game is very good for understanding how the same vowels can make different sounds depending on which letter comes next. If you have **"STO"** and you only hear the short "O" sound, as in "STOP," you won't think of the silent E "O" sound, as in "STONE." Of course, it isn't called Magic E anymore. It's a split digraph, and they won't shut up about it.

NOW TRY THIS

- If you don't want to give your memory a workout, you can write down the letters as you go.

25. Top Ten of Everything

PLAYERS	DIFFICULTY	TIME
1+	Easy	30 mins per list

IN SHORT: List making is more fun than it should be.
Use my categories to list your favorites.

TAGS:
CONVERSATION,
COLLABORATIVE,
WIND-DOWN

WHAT YOU'LL NEED

These are optional:

- Access to the Internet (for research).

- Pen and paper.

HOW TO PLAY

For some reason, the world loves lists—especially countdowns. The Internet is full of them. I spend my life trying to work out what sneaks into my top ten of various categories. Let's not question why this is true and just enjoy the process. Play this one when you're over halfway through your vacation and have run out of things to get excited about.

To play this game, first decide on a category. You could use anything from pages 251–52, one of your own, or any of these fun things to rank:

- Places I've been

- Films I've seen

- Superheroes

- Birthdays I've had

- Smells

- Books I've read

- Sounds

- Flavors of chips

- Accents

- Words in the English language

- Songs

If you're playing this on the go, a top five should be enough to keep in your head. If you have a notepad on your phone or a pen and paper, you could stretch to ten or more.

Each player could make their own list, but it's more fun to make one list among all the players. The second is more difficult but more rewarding, because if you want one particular flavor of chips to be higher up the list, you'll have to make a case for it. Give good enough reasons, argue your point persuasively, and the other players are sure to agree with you, and that's a great feeling!

TIP

- It's best not to make this game too personal; for example, using a category like "favorite people." Believe it or not, there's no joy in finding out that you either have, or haven't, made it into somebody's list of best friends.

FOLLOW UP

- Once you've made your list, make a proper chart with pictures, explanations, and the reasons why each option placed where it did.

- Whoop whoop! Nerd alert! If I were playing this game with a lot of people, I'd encourage everyone to write down their own list, then collect them and make an overall table by using each list as a set of votes. Award 10 points for first place, 9 for second place, etc., and finish with a big overall league table. Mmm. League tables.

26. Story Tornado

PLAYERS	DIFFICULTY	TIME
2+	**Medium**	**5 mins per story**

IN SHORT: Improvise a story with the ingredients that are constantly being thrown at you.

TAGS: STORYTELLING, COLLABORATIVE, CREATIVE

WHAT YOU'LL NEED

- Story ingredients (see pages 231–42) photocopied/ written out and cut out, if you can. You could even add your own ideas! If you don't have time to prepare this in advance, you can just choose the options directly from the back of the book.

- If you've cut out the story ingredients, you'll also need four containers (hats, bowls, shoes) to put them in. Put each category of story ingredients—character, place, object, action—into a separate container.

HOW TO PLAY

This is a chaotic storytelling game. It's an absolute romp, and quite hard at first, but stick with it and you'll create some amazing stories.

One player, the tornado, hands another player, the storyteller, a card from one of the four pots, or just reads a random item from any of the story ingredient pages. It really doesn't matter which one. The tornado may root around and look for a card she wants, or just pick the top one out. Decide beforehand which you'll do and just go with it.

With this one ingredient, the storyteller begins telling his story. Almost immediately, the tornado throws the storyteller another card from a different pot (once again, random or chosen). The storyteller must build this new ingredient into the story and continue.

The game continues, with the tornado adding story ingredients whenever she wants. She can deprive the storyteller of ingredients and watch him improvise with the parts he has, or add more and more until the story's ready to burst.

At some point, the story should end, and then it's time to swap roles.

EXAMPLE

The tornado gives the storyteller a card that says "Dog."
Storyteller: *"Once upon a time there was a dog called Buster."*
The tornado gives the storyteller a card that says "Balloon."
Storyteller: *"He loved chasing balloons so much that his owner only had to blow up a balloon and throw it into the garden, and he'd be out there for hours."*
The tornado gives the storyteller a card that says "Palace."
Storyteller: *"One day, Buster chased a balloon all the way through town and up the steps of the royal palace, and straight through the front door. The queen screamed as the dirty dog walked muddy paw-prints all across their precious rug."*
Etc.

TIPS

- If you're telling the story, pay attention: as with every story, decide who's the main character nice and early, then give that character a problem that they have to solve and make the rest of the story about solving that problem. No matter what the other player gives you, don't abandon the main character and their problem. How can the new ingredients help to further that story?

- If you're the tornado, listen to the storyteller and try to help! Does he sound like he needs a new location? Is the character already laden with objects? It's fun to make it hard for the storyteller, but don't make it impossible!

27. Stupid Superheroes

PLAYERS	DIFFICULTY	TIME
1+	Medium	1 hour +

IN SHORT: Develop your own team of pathetic superheroes—or even worse, supervillains—then battle them against each other!

TAGS:
CREATIVE,
WRITING,
COLLABORATIVE,
CONVERSATION

WHAT YOU'LL NEED

- Paper and pencil.

- Colored pencils, felt tips, or a drawing app on a tablet.

- "Object" story suggestions (see pages 237–39), ideally photocopied/ written out and cut out, though you can just choose them from the back of the book.

HOW TO PLAY

This one's great to play at a table. It will turn any long afternoon into an absolute feast of creativity. Each player should shuffle the "object" story suggestions, then pick one, or just choose randomly from the list at the back (close your eyes and point). This item becomes the source of the superpower for a brand-new superhero or supervillain. Choose an element of that object that might be useful for fighting crime or, if you feel a little villainous, for causing it. Before you share your idea, give yourself five minutes to answer these questions in your head, or on some scrap paper:

- **What is your character's name?** It could include the word on your card plus -man, -woman, -boy, or -girl. Alternatively, go a little more creative.

- **Hero or villain?**

- **What is your character's real-life identity?** What do they do when they're not dressed in Lycra? How old/young/rich/poor/happy/sad/

popular/unpopular are they in real life? Do they have a job or family? You need to decide.

- **What, exactly, is your character's special power?** What can he/she do that's completely unique and new? HINT: think about the unique qualities of the item you picked. Shooting _____ out of his/her hands is not a new idea. Use it only if you must!

- **How did your character get their power?** You've got to have an origin story. If you're stuck, "Bitten by a radioactive _____" is a great place to start.

- **What is your character's weakness?** Every superhero has a weakness. It's normally the opposite of the thing on your card, or the thing that would destroy the thing on your card.

The best players will not make the strongest superhero, but the most original one. Superman may have cool pants, but someone has already created him and even the first one is boring. Be original!

Now it's time to share your characters. In turn, tell the other players all about your superhero. Try to keep it fun, and give as much detail as you can without being boring. If you're on your own, don't worry! Skip to the next step.

Try asking questions about the other players' characters to get a little deeper into their heads. If they can transform into a jellyfish, how long does it take? And what if they're on land when it happens? And do they also get the intelligence of a jellyfish? Pretend this is actually taking place in real life, and work out the kinks of the character.

Here's where you get creative. There are a few options as to what happens next:

1. Every player can draw/write the scene when the characters meet (and do battle) for the first time. Who wins is up to them, but think it out first. You can do this as one big action page, or use a comic-book grid to show the sequence of events.

2. Role-play the characters and make up a conversation between them. Would they team up or fight? What common ground do they have? Would they be a successful team?

3. Have each player judge who would win in a fight. You each have one minute to tell the story of how you think the fight would go, and who would end up on top.

4. If you're feeling artistic, draw your character, stick the paper onto a thick card, and cut it out with an extra flap at the bottom so they can stand up. Once you've done a few, you'll have your own superhero team right there in front of you. This can be the base for excellent written stories, photo comics, tabletop games, or just a cool display.

EXAMPLE

If the object card says "cheese":

Name: *Doctor Roquefort (villain).*

Real-life identity: *Robert Camembert, a gray-haired brain surgeon from Paris. He lives alone (because he smells so strongly of cheese) and no longer works at the hospital after his brain surgery patients woke up and complained about the stink.*

Power: *He can melt into a pool of cheese and move about as a liquid. His ripe dairy smell is another element of his power, but not a particularly useful one.*

Origin story: *Robert Camembert left a particularly strong French cheese out of the fridge for weeks, and then ate a mouthful. Little did he know that the cheese had begun to rot and evolved a dangerous DNA-editing strain of bacteria, which turned him into the monstrosity that he is today.*

Weakness: *Any source of heat can begin to trigger his melting power, which can be awkward on a summer's day or on the bus. When in his liquid state, even though he can slip between prison bars and squeeze inside locked safes, he is both delicious and spreadable. Also people can smell him coming from half a mile away because, well, he stinks.*

NOW TRY THIS

• If you really, really like a character, use it as a basis to get started on a graphic novel! I cannot wait to see what you create.

28. What's It Worth?

PLAYERS	DIFFICULTY	TIME
2+	Medium	10 mins per item

IN SHORT: Find an object lying around. Pretend to be an expert on it. This game is very, very silly.

TAGS: CREATIVE, CONVERSATION, SILLY

WHAT YOU'LL NEED

- Any weird and wonderful items from around the world.

HOW TO PLAY

This game uses items that you find on vacation, or just around your house, and turns them into pieces of rare and magnificent antiquity.

Before you play this game, it might be worth watching an episode of *Antiques Roadshow*, or a few clips on YouTube. Watch how the experts talk in detail about the piece's history, its use, its maker, the materials, etc. Look at their passion and love for the item, and the way they talk with such enthusiasm.

One player hands the "expert" an object. It could be anything, but the stranger the better.

If the expert knows what this thing is, he should immediately pretend it's something else. If it's a pot, turn it upside down and now it's a hat! If it's a bulldog clip, now it's a bullfrog clip, used for catching frogs between its pincers.

The expert must talk for a given amount of time (e.g., two minutes) about this item. Of course, he'll need to make up everything about it. If he gets stuck, use these questions for inspiration:

- What is this item used for?

- What special features does it have?

- When/where was it made?

- Which company/craftsman made it? How?

- How rare/old/unusual is this item?

- What is the history of items like this? Were they popular, and with whom?

- And finally . . . what's it worth?

TIPS

- If you get stuck, spend some time describing how beautiful and exquisite the item is. The experts on *Antiques Roadshow really* love their antiques.

- If you're the listener and the expert is getting stuck, ask some leading questions from the list above.

29. Genre Bender

PLAYERS	DIFFICULTY	TIME
2	Hard	20 mins

IN SHORT: Storytelling game with a big twist.

TAGS:
STORYTELLING,
COLLABORATIVE,
SILLY

WHAT YOU'LL NEED

- Nothing at all.

HOW TO PLAY

This game can't be won or lost, but it's a huge amount of fun, so isn't everyone the winner? One player, the storyteller, begins to tell the other a story. For this, choose any story you like from a book, TV, film, or stage. You could even choose one of my story titles or opening lines on pages 243–50.

Before you begin, the players should discuss which genre this story belongs to. A genre is the category that the story fits into. Here are the main options:

- **Horror:** Scary, creepy stories with lots of suspense.

- **Mystery:** A story where the main character, and the reader, attempts to solve a mysterious crime.

- **Sci-Fi:** Anything futuristic or in space, with aliens, lasers, or time travel.

- **Fantasy:** Set in a made-up world with magic, dragons, kings, and queens.

- **Romance:** A story where the characters struggle to find their true love.

- **Comedy:** Jokes, funny characters, and slapstick moments.

- **Drama:** A real-life tale about school, family, and the modern world.

- **Fairy tale:** Talking animals, princesses in castles, cute gnomes, and evil witches.

- **Myth/legend:** Ancient tales of gods and long journeys, big battles, and magical beasts.

Now, at any point during the story, the listener may call, "Change to _____," and decide on a new genre for the story. The storyteller must continue in the new genre.

The game ends when the story ends!

EXAMPLE

Storyteller: *"Harry Potter was a normal boy who lived with his mean uncle and aunt, until Hagrid the giant told him he was a wizard."*
Listener: *"Change to fairy tale."*
Storyteller: *"Hagrid and Harry went into the forest and found a talking fox. 'I'm better at magic tricks than you!' said the fox."*
Listener: *"Change to horror."*
Storyteller: *"Harry's eyes widened as he saw that the fox was holding a tiny knife. 'My first trick,' said the fox, 'is to make blood spring from your chest!'"*
Listener: *"Change to fantasy."*
Storyteller: *"Harry grabbed his magical amulet and held it up to the sun. From the distance, his dragon roared, the beats of its wing shaking leaves from the trees. The fox turned to flee."*
Listener: *"Change to romance."*
Storyteller: *"'Stop!' cried Harry. 'Don't leave yet!' The dragon landed nearby with a dozen red roses in its beak. 'I have something to tell you. Something . . . important . . .' Harry whispered."*
Etc.

TIP

- The more times you switch genres, the more complicated the story will get. Don't worry, though! This game is supposed to be silly.

30. Avagat

PLAYERS	DIFFICULTY	TIME
2+	**Hard**	**Learn in 30 mins, use for life**

IN SHORT: An excellent secret language where the words hide in plain sight.

TAGS: SILLY, GRAMMAR, CONVERSATION, LONG-TERM

WHAT YOU'LL NEED

- Nothing at all.

HOW TO PLAY

Hevege-llovogo. Myvygy navagame ivigis Ivigi-vavagan.

"Avagat" is a secret language that my sisters used to employ to speak to each other. It completely baffled me for years, but once I worked it out (or once they told me . . . I don't remember . . .), I felt thoroughly "in" on the secret. It's a great one to use on vacation, when you can pretend to be speaking in a "foreign" language, then switch back to immaculate English and confuse onlookers. Also, it takes time to perfect, so airport waiting rooms or long car journeys are the ideal time to practice.

I'll teach you how to use this language, but be aware of how inclusive/exclusive you're being. Half of the fun with a secret language is to see if others can work out what you're saying, though do bear in mind (and this is from experience) that it can be *quite* annoying if you're the one who's not in on the secret.

So here's how it works.

Take any word and break it down into syllables. A syllable is a part of the word that takes one "beat."

So, for example, **"Hello"** has two syllables. **He-llo**. **"Octopus"** has three. **Oc-to-pus.** Tap along with your word to get better at identifying syllables.

Now, with each syllable of your word, you need to interrupt the vowel with the consonants **v** and **g**. So the "ah" noise would be "avagah" and the "ee" noise would be "evegee."

He-llo now becomes **Hevege-llovogo**.

Octopus now becomes **Ovogoc-tovogo-puvugus**.

Now, this all sounds very weird, but with practice you'll not only be able to speak Avagat, but also understand it when others speak it. For a language where the real words are right there but hidden by lots of Vs and Gs, it's pretty hard to decipher if you don't know the rule!

If you want to practice, I recommend trying to recite the alphabet. I've tried to spell these out as best I can. The rest you'll have to do yourself. Sorry . . .

Avagay, bevegey, cevegey, devegey, evegey, evegef, geevegey, ayvagaych, ivigiy, etc. Good luck!

Novogow. Dovogoo youvugu uvugun-deveger-stavagand whavagat ivigiy avagam savagay-iviging?

CHAPTER 4
ONE-ON-ONE

It's rare that you get to spend time with just one person, whether it's your significant other, sibling, parent, offspring, friend, or cat. Even when you do come together, usually there are plenty of reasons to ignore each other: smartphones, chores, TV to catch up on. Much better to separate yourselves between the large pages of a newspaper or the glare of a screen, so that you're basically alone but sitting in the same room.

But maybe, just occasionally, you should make the effort to come together properly. Or, perhaps there's a specific situation where you need to pass time with someone: you both have a long train journey to fill, or you're waiting for the doctor to examine your daughter's blocked ear and it looks like it'll be a long one. A long wait, not a long ear. Obviously.

Whatever the case, these one-on-one games are perfect for those moments. They're duels or challenges that require conversation or tit-for-tat interaction, helping you make the most of your time together. They're also silly amounts of fun.

Many of the games in this chapter require a notebook and pencil, so they might be ones to play at home. But if you know ahead of time that you'll be sitting somewhere for a long while, why not pack these in your bag? If you're really keen, get your hands on a mini-whiteboard and some dry-erase markers from a stationery shop, and you'll have unlimited paper for life.

31. Reflect Me

PLAYERS	DIFFICULTY	TIME
2+	**Easy**	**5 mins**

IN SHORT: Explore reflection in this quiet, collaborative game that produces fun drawings!

TAGS: ARTSY, WIND-DOWN, MATH

WHAT YOU'LL NEED

- Whiteboard and dry-erase markers, ideally, but scrap paper and pencils will do.

HOW TO PLAY

Take your paper and lay it landscape (wider than it is tall). Now, draw a dotted line down the middle of the page so that you have two equal segments.

One player is the leader, and the other is the follower. You can swap roles every round, so don't worry about who goes first.

The leader draws a line, or a simple squiggle, on their side of the board. Next, the follower copies that mark on their side of the board as if it's reflected in the mirror. Remember: when reflected, everything looks the wrong way around.

As the leader adds more lines, the picture becomes more and more complex. If you're the follower, try to be as perfect as possible. Think about exactly where, and exactly what size, your markings should be.

It's the leader's job to notice if the follower has made any mistakes. If you're playing on a whiteboard, these can be corrected easily. The game is over when the follower decides the masterpiece is complete, and then the roles swap.

TIP

- If you need practice on this, find a wall-mounted mirror and wiggle your hands around for a bit. The closer to the mirror you are, the closest to the mirror your reflection is. Use this same principle when reflecting in the dotted line.

NOW TRY THIS

- Once you're really confident in this game, how about agreeing that in each round, the follower will make **one intentional mistake**. The leader will have to pay attention to make sure that they don't miss the mistake. This works well because it's easy for the leader to lose concentration and just focus on their own half. We don't want that!

- There's another game in this, which takes place in real life rather than on a whiteboard. Sit or stand face-to-face and imagine a mirror separating you and your partner. One player is the leader, the other the reflection. Every move the leader makes (slowly at first) the reflection should copy, as exactly as possible. See how accurately you can mirror your partner. After a few minutes, swap roles.

32. Blindfold Game

PLAYERS	DIFFICULTY	TIME
2	Easy	30 mins

IN SHORT: An instructions game to be played around the house.

TAGS:
COLLABORATIVE,
VOCABULARY,
AROUND THE
HOUSE

WHAT YOU'LL NEED

- A blindfold. This could be a scarf, a shirt, or any material that blocks your view and can be tied safely around your head without blocking your mouth.

HOW TO PLAY

This game is perfect for two players at home, because it morphs a place you thought you knew well into a mystery maze, just by eliminating one of the senses. However, don't play this in a public place, for obvious reasons.

One player, the listener, puts on the blindfold and the other player, the commander, decides on a place for the listener to go.

The commander must give clear, simple instructions to get the listener from point to point. This may include number of steps, angle and direction of turns, and even movements to open and close doors.

The commander is not allowed to touch the listener to direct her, nor is he allowed to intentionally direct her into any walls, however funny that is.

IMPORTANT

- Don't even attempt to lead the listener down any stairs. Going up stairs is possible but difficult, but never, ever go down.

- Don't direct the listener near anything that could hurt them.

- If you're wearing the blindfold, never take risks.

NOW TRY THIS

- Once you've become a blindfold-game expert, how about stacking up the instructions? The commander could give three or more instructions at a time, for example, "Take three steps forward, then turn left, then reach forward and grab the handle." After this, the listener must carry out the instructions while the commander must not intervene (unless the listener is putting themselves in danger). The added challenge here is that the commander can't keep making small adjustments, hence small mistakes from the listener may lead them way off course.

33. Squiggle Challenge

PLAYERS	DIFFICULTY	TIME
1+	Easy	10 mins

IN SHORT: Idle drawing game with hilarious consequences.

TAGS: CREATIVE, WIND-DOWN, ARTSY

YOU WILL NEED

• Paper and colored pencils.

HOW TO PLAY

This is kind of a one-player game, but you really need somebody to set it up for you. If there are two of you, why not set up each other's squiggles at the same time?

Have somebody draw you a squiggle on a piece of paper. It can be any shape or size, but keep it simple. Too much detail at this point can make the game very hard!

Now look at your squiggle from every angle and decide what it could be. When you're ready, go ahead and continue the drawing. The weirder the better!

TIP

• Avoid faces. Any squiggle could become a face. Start by asking yourself, "What else in the world has this shape?" Then just go for it.

NOW TRY THIS

• If you have access to a scanner or photocopier, why not copy the same squiggle and give everybody the same one? It will be fascinating to see how different each person's drawing ends up.

34. Fortunately/Unfortunately

PLAYERS	DIFFICULTY	TIME
2	Easy	10 mins per round

IN SHORT: Storytelling game where two players battle it out to make things great/terrible for the main character.

TAGS:
VOCABULARY,
AROUND THE
HOUSE, SILLY

WHAT YOU'LL NEED

- Nothing at all.

HOW TO PLAY

I've said that this works for two players, but it's easy to adapt for more. It's certainly worth a go, however many people are sitting around.

One player starts with an **opening sentence of a story**. It could be anything, but if you're stuck, why not use one of the 100 suggestions starting on page 246?

Then, the next player adds the second sentence of the story, but begins his sentence with "Unfortunately." In other words, he's going to make things bad for the main character.

However, now the first player steps in with her sentence, which must begin with "Fortunately." She's going to improve things for the main character ... until the other player begins the next sentence with "Unfortunately."

This carries on until one player runs out of ideas, or both get bored. It makes some amazingly dramatic stories.

EXAMPLE

Player 1: *"Timmy lived by the sea, and wanted to be an explorer."*
Player 2: *"Unfortunately, he didn't have a boat."*
Player 1: *"Fortunately, he saw a competition in the local paper, where the prize was a boat!"*
Player 2: *"Unfortunately, he had missed the entry deadline."*

Player 1: *"Fortunately, so had everybody else, so his entry won the competition!"*
Player 2: *"Unfortunately, his prize was a tiny toy boat."*
Player 1: *"Fortunately, Timmy was also tiny, so it was the perfect size."*
Etc.

TIP

- It can be difficult to balance making things good/bad for your character without just ruining the story. "Unfortunately, Timmy drowned" would not be a good move. Try: "Unfortunately, a giant wave knocked Timmy from his boat." In the second case, at least Timmy (and therefore the other player) has a chance. Remember, you're telling a story, not playing chess. You don't necessarily want to ruin your opponent's chance to save things.

NOW TRY THIS

- As I say, it's possible to include more players. If there are an odd number of players, you will find that each time it's your turn, you have to be first kind, then mean, then kind to your character. It's a very different game this way!

35. Control the Robot

PLAYERS	DIFFICULTY	TIME
2	Easy	30 mins

IN SHORT: A silly movement game in which you practice giving clear instructions.

TAGS: COLLABORATIVE, ACTIVE, AROUND THE HOUSE

WHAT YOU'LL NEED

* Nothing at all.

HOW TO PLAY

This game is great when two of you are bored at home, and for practicing giving instructions that deal with movement.

One player is the robot, and the other is its creator. **The robot must follow every instruction given by its creator.**

The creator should decide on a simple task that he wants the robot to complete. It could be making a sandwich, brushing her teeth, feeding the cat, or any other number of random chores.

The creator then begins giving simple, clear instructions. It is the robot's job to take the instructions completely literally. If told to "walk forward," the robot should walk until she hits a wall and carry on walking. If told to "turn left," the robot should continually turn left in a circle until told to stop.

If told to do anything complicated (e.g., "Go upstairs"), the robot should turn to the creator and announce in her robotic voice, "Bleep, bloop, does not compute." She'll need much clearer and simpler instructions than that: something like "Lift your left leg and place it on the stair in front."

(In a somewhat legendary round of this game at school—where I was the teacher, but in this case, also the robot—a few unclear instructions led to a piece of jammy bread being stuck on the classroom ceiling. Don't make my mistakes, folks.)

After the task is completed, swap roles and try a new task.

TIPS

- If you're the robot and feel like you aren't getting precise enough instructions, don't break character to complain about it. Instead, say something like "Bleep, bloop, further data required," or "Query: direction of walking unclear. Awaiting input." They'll get the idea soon enough.

- Similarly, if you're the creator and the robot doesn't seem to be following instructions, or is getting things wrong on purpose, make a big performance of tutting, complaining about malfunctions, then turning the robot off and on again. If that doesn't work, unplug him at the wall and call the manufacturer.

- If the robot feels uncomfortable at any point, stop the game and talk about it. The robot should never feel forced to do anything.

- Likewise, the creator should never direct the robot toward situations that might be dangerous, and the robot should not agree to go toward anything dangerous. Just use your (human) brain!

36. Boxes

PLAYERS	DIFFICULTY	TIME
2	Easy	20 mins

IN SHORT: Add a line to a grid, trying to complete boxes while stopping your opponent from doing the same.

TAGS: STRATEGY, PASS THE TIME, WIND-DOWN, MATH

WHAT YOU'LL NEED

• Graph paper, or normal paper (it will be a tiny bit harder to draw the dots, but not by much).

• Pencil or pen (two different colors is fun but not necessary).

HOW TO PLAY

Start by drawing a five-by-five (for a quick game) or ten-by-ten (for a longer game) grid of dots on your paper. Make sure to space them out evenly, and make sure that they're in line with each other. If you have graph paper, then it's easy: draw a dot every time the lines cross. If you have lined or blank paper, just try to make it as neat as possible. Your complete grid should look like this:

Now the game begins. Take turns joining two adjacent dots with a horizontal or vertical line. **No diagonals allowed.**

The aim of the game is to be the person to draw the fourth line around a box, which would complete it. But obviously, since you're taking turns, if you leave a box with three lines complete, your opponent can finish it. So be careful! Unless you want to take a risk, make sure that no box has more than two complete lines around it.

Eventually, though, it will become impossible to add another line without giving your opponent the chance to complete a box. In this example, Player B has run out of options and has been forced to put a third line around a box at the bottom of the grid:

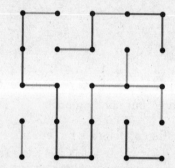

Player A can now draw the final line to complete that box, write the initial of his name inside, and then **he gets to move again immediately**. Because of this, it's possible to have a string of turns when all your opponent can do is watch as you complete a chain of boxes. Player A will be able to complete the box above it, too. Anticipating this, and trying to avoid giving your opponent a glut of boxes, is part of the game.

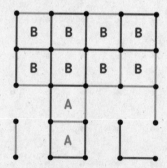

In this example, B gave A two boxes, but A added a line that let B take eight boxes in one turn. Soon you'll learn to see chain reactions like this before they happen. Once the entire grid is complete, add up your boxes and see who has more. They win the round!

37. Dice Soccer

PLAYERS	DIFFICULTY	TIME
2	Medium	**15 mins per match**

IN SHORT: Take on your partner in an exciting soccer simulation game.

WHAT YOU'LL NEED

- A piece of paper to draw your soccer field.
- A coin or counter to represent the ball.
- Two dice (but one will do).

TAGS:
COMPETITIVE,
MATH

HOW TO PLAY

Tabletop gaming is a fantastic way to pass the time. I've become fascinated by the use of dice to simulate fantasy worlds and epic battles or, in this case, a soccer match. This version of **Dice Soccer** is simple to pick up and diverting enough to keep you playing for ages. The huge dose of luck makes for exciting games.

Here is a simple diagram of the field that you'll want to draw on your piece of paper. Notice the six segments of the field (three on each side of the center circle, including the penalty area). Leave space for somewhere to write the score and the match clock tally (currently "0").

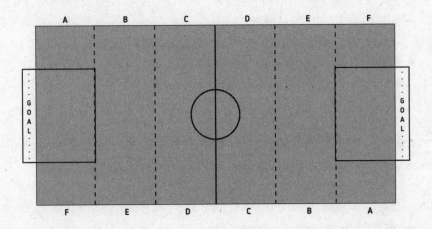

Place the paper lengthwise between yourself and your opponent. You will each be defending your own "end" nearest to you and aiming forward. To begin the game, both players roll a die, and the player with the higher score places the ball in their version of segment C. **Notice that for each player, segment C is in a different place, as the segments go in opposite orders, depending on which direction you are heading.** If the rolls are level, roll again. Play then begins.

To score a goal, you'll have to get the ball, progress through to segment F, and score in the goal.

When in control of the ball, the player must roll a die to see what happens next. Here's what happens when the ball is in each segment.

Segments A to E:

First, the player **without the ball** rolls their die to defend. Then, the player **with the ball** rolls to beat that score.

- If the player with the ball wins by 2 or more: Long pass. (Move forward two segments, or one if you are already in segment E.) The player keeps possession.
- If the player with the ball wins by 1: Short pass. (Move forward one segment.) The player keeps possession.
- If both players get the same score: Add up the scores of the two dice and add it to the match clock tally at the top of your page. So if you both roll a 5, add ten minutes to the match clock tally. The player keeps possession.
- If the player with the ball loses by 1: Back pass. (Move back one segment, if you can.) However, the player keeps possession.
- If the player with the ball loses by 2 or more: Tackle. (Ball stays where it is, but your opponent gains possession.)

Segment F (Penalty Area):

This one is a little different. The player **with the ball** should call out a number between 1 and 6, then roll. The defender can't do anything now!

- If the number they roll is the same as the number they called: Goal! (Add 1 to your score and your opponent gains possession, and kicks off in their version of segment C.)

- If the number they roll is 1 away from the number they called: Rebound! (Roll again.)
- Otherwise: Saved! (Your opponent gains possession in their own segment A.)

The player with the ball advances and advances until they lose possession of the ball in one of the ways described above. As soon as this happens, the game changes direction. **Make sure you are using the letters on your side**, not your opponent's.

The match clock ticks on as you roll doubles (see above). When it hits ninety minutes, the game is over. If it's a draw, why not play "Next Goal Wins" to decide it?

NOW TRY THIS

- You could definitely make this game more complicated, if that's your thing. You could rewrite the scores to include fouls, corners, free kicks, and penalties. If you create a set of rules that works really well, tell me! I'm always keen to hear new rules.

- I'm a big fan of league tables. If there are lots of you involved, make a quick round robin tournament where everyone plays everyone. Three points for a win, one for a draw, and nothing for a loss. The two highest points scorers could have a final playoff at the end, to decide the ultimate **Dice Soccer** champ.

38. Switch!

PLAYERS	DIFFICULTY	TIME
2	Medium	15 mins

IN SHORT: Storytelling game with a big twist.

TAGS:
STORYTELLING,
COLLABORATIVE,
SILLY

WHAT YOU'LL NEED

• Nothing at all.

HOW TO PLAY

One player, the storyteller, begins to tell the listener a story. For this, you could begin with a fairy tale that you both know, or the plot of a book you have both read or a film you have both seen.

Some stories you could use:

• *Goldilocks and the Three Bears*

• *Rapunzel*

• *Snow White and the Seven Dwarves*

• *Hansel and Gretel*

• *The Three Billy Goats Gruff*

• *Cinderella*

• *The Gingerbread Man*

At any point, the listener can yell "SWITCH!" and whatever the storyteller is currently saying, she must change it to the absolute opposite and continue the story in this new direction.

The storyteller can choose to end the story whenever she likes, but it's likely that it won't end up as she'd imagined. This improvisation and going with the flow is what makes the game great. Don't struggle against it!

EXAMPLE

Storyteller: *"Once upon a time, a young girl called Goldilocks was walking in the forest. She came across a little wooden house and knocked on the door, but nobody was in."*

Listener: *"SWITCH!"*

Storyteller: *"But somebody was in! Daddy Bear opened the door and smiled at Goldilocks. 'We're having porridge,' he said."*

Listener: *"SWITCH!"*

Storyteller: *"'We're not having porridge; we're eating a human. Would you like some?' 'Oh, no thank you!' cried Goldilocks."*

Listener: *"SWITCH!"*

Storyteller: *"'I'd love some!' replied Goldilocks."*

Etc.

TIPS

- You don't have to say "SWITCH!" all the time. Let the storyteller tell the story for a while before picking your moment. You could even limit yourself to three switches per game.

- When I've played this game, I've come across some players being tempted to "work around" the switches and try their hardest to tell the usual story with just a few bumps in the road. So for example, if the storyteller is forced to say that the bears were already in the house, try not to fix it by going on to say "but then the bears went out, leaving the house empty." This game is about seeing how the stories can change, not how good you are at keeping them the same.

- You don't have to use the absolute opposite. The true opposite of porridge is . . . not porridge? The storyteller chose a human because it felt very different from porridge. Have a little freedom with this one.

39. Hangman Mastermind

PLAYERS	DIFFICULTY	TIME
2	Hard	15 mins per word

IN SHORT: Somewhere between Mastermind (the code-cracking board game, not the quiz show) and Hangman. Easy to play, hard to master.

TAGS: SPELLING, STRATEGY, VOCABULARY, COMPETITIVE

WHAT YOU'LL NEED

- Pencil and paper (or mini whiteboard and dry-erase markers).

HOW TO PLAY

This is one of my favorite word games in existence. One player, the judge, picks a four-letter word (no names or abbreviations) and keeps it a secret. The only limitation is that the word cannot have any repeated letters at all (so "kind" is fine, "book" and "none" are not).

The guesser then must write their first four-letter-word guess on the whiteboard. The first player awards them a score: 1 point for every letter that they guessed correctly. The order of the letters is completely ignored; you only get marks based on the letters used.

Using this knowledge, the guesser has another guess, and so on, until they find the word. The aim is to find the word with the fewest possible guesses.

EXAMPLE

The judge has chosen the word "LATE."

Guesser's guess	Points awarded by the judge
PLUM	1
PLAN	2
PAIN	1
LAST	3
TALE	4
LATE	WIN!

TIPS

- It really helps if the guesser keeps an alphabet nearby. Cross off any letters you're sure are not right, circle any letters you know are in the word, and write down any further information you've worked out.

- If you receive 0 points on a guess, that's great! Now you know four letters that cannot be in the word.

- Until you are an expert, try changing one letter at a time. If your score changes, you know exactly which letter made the difference.

- Remember, 4 points does not mean you've won! You may have all the letters, but not in the right order.

BOSS LEVEL

- When you're ready, move on to five-letter words. That's a whole new game, and it's just as much fun, if not more so!

40. Lego Challenge

PLAYERS	DIFFICULTY	TIME
2	Hard	1 hour (at least)

IN SHORT: Instruction and communication game that transforms a well-known toy.

TAGS: VOCABULARY, COLLABORATIVE, WIND-DOWN

WHAT YOU'LL NEED

- A small set of building blocks with instructions. (Lego is one of many types that you could choose.)

HOW TO PLAY

I was taught this game as a teacher under the aspirational name of "Lego Therapy." It's an amazing program that builds communication and social skills for children who struggle with that sort of thing. However, I truly feel that a similar, if simplified, game is a great challenge for anybody. It's also addictive and fun, and a brand-new way of doing Lego!

One player, the instructor, holds the instructions, but may not touch or point to the blocks. Meanwhile, the other player, the builder, may touch and build with the blocks, but not look at the instructions.

Together, they must build the model. The instructor will have to work out how to specify exactly which block to find from the set, and then how to add it to the model. It's really difficult, but any sort of pointing or demonstrating is completely banned. Use color, shape, size, location, and then prepositions such as "under," "above," and "beside" to be really specific about where each piece goes.

The builder will have to listen really carefully, and prepare to be wrong many, many times! Both players will need to be patient.

It's worth trying this game at least twice, so you can play both roles. There are challenges for each.

TIPS

- One important bit of admin between instructor and builder will be what to call each type of brick. You could go mathematical ("two rows of five blobs, thin yellow rectangle"), freestyle ("a kinda squat, flat banana piece"), or relational ("same as you used for the propeller, but yellow"). Develop your own style and stick with it. Develop a shared language. Whatever you do, don't operate your builder like a fairground-crane game. ("Left arm toward you, down a bit, up a bit, grab that piece. No, the other one.") This is not the way to play.

- If you're the instructor, you're going to be really tempted to intervene, but don't. Sit on your hands and think about how you can be more specific. If the builder isn't getting it, it's more likely that you're not being clear enough than that they aren't listening properly.

NOW TRY THIS

- If there are three of you, how about having one person as an instructor, one seeker who finds the pieces, and one as the builder. Make sure to rotate the roles nice and often.

CHAPTER 5
PARTY TIME

Parties. They're supposed to be fun—and they are, when you're not in charge. When it's your house, or when you've hired the hall, it's an absolute nightmare. Who's eaten all the cocktail sausages? Who keeps leaving wineglasses in perilous positions hanging over the new carpet? Who fed the dog a double gin and tonic? Which party animal switched the music playlist from Tchaikovsky to techno?

Whether it's a party for kids or adults, hosting one is a bit like herding cats. If anything, a party will leave you more scratched and covered in hair than cat herding, and you still won't have herded any of those cats. So what's the solution? How do you make a party an enjoyable experience?

This chapter holds the answer. It's chock-full of party games to play with any excitable group. You've got all-ages games, silly circle games, and psychological setups that'll have you suspecting everyone. They're all engaging and exciting enough to feel like a real highlight of your party.

Read through this chapter before a party, not during. Select one game that will suit the people present, and make sure you know the rules so that you can explain them nicely and simply to your assembled guests. This is especially true for **Mafia**, an absolutely incredible game that does require the host to know the rules pretty well before you start. It's worth it, though!

41. Clap Clap SQUAWK

PLAYERS	DIFFICULTY	TIME
As many as possible, really	**Easy**	**10 mins**

IN SHORT: Tap into your spirit animals with this rowdy variation of a naming game.

WHAT YOU'LL NEED

TAGS: MEMORY, SILLY, CIRCLE GAMES, RHYTHM

- Nothing at all.

HOW TO PLAY

This game works best with more people: four is fine, but it won't be as much fun as with nine-plus.

First of all, every player should pick an animal, and an action that is associated with that animal. Once you've all picked, share it with the group. Make your action really recognizable. A cat licking its paw, an eagle beating its wings, or a squid squirting ink might be good examples. The whole group should have a go at each other's noises/actions too, to get used to them.

To begin the game, the group gets a good, slow tapping rhythm going. Pat your lap or gently clap, trying not to speed up (yet). The rhythm should be the same as the introduction to "We Will Rock You," but much slower.

Clap—Clap—TAP. Clap—Clap—TAP.

One player starts, on a **TAP**, by doing the action of one of the other players. Perhaps another player chose a lion's roar, so the first player does this action, effectively passing the game over to the lion. Now it is the lion's turn to instantly pick someone else's action. On the next **TAP**, the lion does the kangaroo's action, which is bouncy and probably involves boxing. Next, the kangaroo does an elephant squirting water from its trunk, which passes the game to the elephant, etc.

If any player misses their turn, or fails to do the action of somebody who's still in the game, then they are eliminated.

One by one, the players drop out, until two remain. You could leave it here, proclaiming the two last players joint champions, or have them duke it out in the final round. Unfortunately, the final round is pretty easy, because you only need to remember one animal impression. One way to solve this is to gently speed up as you play, which often leads to some very silly things occurring.

This game is best when played multiple times, because in the second game you've all got to pick fresh animals. NO REPEATS! Not only do your impressions get stranger, but also you've still got a whole zoo full of animals squawking about in your head that you might accidentally select when it's your turn. Do you have a good enough selective memory to forget each player's previous animal impression, and remember the new one?

TIPS

- Make your animal actions simple and full of movement. An impression of a bunny twitching her little nose, no matter how adorable, looks much like somebody working back a sneeze. You could do an impression of a bunny leaping over a tuft of grass instead. The more creative, the better.

- If you're playing this in public, be aware of others. You have a responsibility to not annoy them, even if your animal impressions are really, *really* good.

42. Zip Bong

PLAYERS	DIFFICULTY	TIME
6-15	Easy	10 mins per round

IN SHORT: A game full of silly noises and thinking under pressure.

TAGS: COMPETITIVE, RHYTHM, MEMORY, CIRCLE GAMES

WHAT YOU'LL NEED

- Nothing at all.

HOW TO PLAY

Sit in a circle with your hands together, as if in prayer. Make sure that your lips cover your teeth, so that no white is showing. This may sound strange, but it's vitally important!

One player (let's say the youngest) points their hands toward the person to their left and says, "Zip."

The person to the first player's left then does the same, saying, "Zip."

The "Zip" passes clockwise around the circle, each player moving their hands and saying their "Zip," all without showing their teeth.

At any point, a player may pass the sound back to their right, moving their hand in that direction and saying, "Bong." The "Bong" sound then travels counterclockwise for a while, until somebody changes it back to "Zip" and it goes clockwise again.

So, whenever you pass to your left, it's **"Zip."** Whenever you pass to your right, it's **"Bong."**

The game is all about following the rules. You are eliminated if:

- You pass the sound left but say "Bong."

- You pass the sound right but say "Zip."

- You make any noise at all when it isn't your turn.

- You make no noise when it is your turn.

- You show your teeth.

The last rule is the odd one out. It's there because it's really hard to say "Zip" with your lips over your teeth, which makes people laugh, which makes them show their teeth, which makes them get eliminated.

Each time someone is eliminated, the person whose turn it would have been after that takes their turn.

When it's down to two, the players stand face-to-face and still pass the noise left or right, not directly forward. Every other player should watch that they are making the right noises with the right movements, as the players get faster and faster. At this stage, though, what'll probably win or lose it is laughing.

The game ends when only one person remains. They are the **Zip Bong** champion!

. . . Until the next round.

TIP

- Watch the "zzz" of zip! It's easy to show your teeth, but there are ways around it.

NOW TRY THIS

- Another way to play this is that "Zip" continues the previous direction and "Bong" changes direction, but after that it's back to "Zip" again, even if traveling counterclockwise. Make sure everybody knows which you're doing before you start, though! We don't want to cause a bongument.

43. Bang!

PLAYERS	DIFFICULTY	TIME
8-30	Easy	15 mins

IN SHORT: Nonverbal circle game based on reaction times and quick thinking.

TAGS: COMPETITIVE, ACTIVE, CIRCLE GAMES

WHAT YOU'LL NEED

• Nothing at all.

HOW TO PLAY

Stand in a circle and clasp your hands together with the index and middle fingers facing forward, so that you've got a finger gun. It's loaded, so be careful.

One player begins by pointing clearly at another in the circle and shooting, by shouting, **"BANG!"**

The target must instantly duck to avoid the bullet, while the two players on either side of the target must turn toward each other and shoot their finger guns, shouting, "BANG!"

Essentially, three things can happen:

1. The target of the original "BANG" doesn't react in time, and either of the players on either side shoot him before he ducks down. The original target has been shot and is eliminated.

2. The target of the first "BANG" ducks in time to avoid the bullet, and the players on either side shoot. The last of those two players to say "BANG!" has been shot and is eliminated. If it's a dead draw (pardon the pun) and the two guns are shot at *exactly* the same time, then the original shooter gets another shot at a new target.

3. One of the players says the wrong thing, or jumps instead of ducks, or turns the wrong way, or forgets to do anything at all because he's thinking about lizards. This player has been shot and is eliminated.

When you have been eliminated, you must sit down and enjoy the rest of the game.

Now, the successful shooter (the one whose shot eliminated the last player) gets to choose a new target and shoot. The game continues.

It becomes interesting at this point for those still standing, because the players next to them will gradually change, so they need to react in new ways when people get shot. When it is your turn and you get to choose whom to shoot, **you may not shoot the person next to you**. When there are only three players left, you will find that you have to, so at this point it's fine! This rule helps to avoid people cheating by shooting the person next to them and then instantly "reacting" by shooting again to win the round. If this doesn't make sense, try it and see.

It's particularly complicated when you get down to three players, because whomever gets shot, everyone has to do something. When you get down to two players, however, you'll have to do something new:

Duel

The two remaining players stand back to back with their finger guns raised. One player who has already been eliminated slowly lists the names of fruit, and for every fruit, the two duelists take one step away from each other. When the player says the name of a vegetable, the two duelists turn and shoot. First to say "BANG!" is the winner!

TIPS

- It's quite useful to have an arbiter in this game: somebody who gets the final decision on who shot first. They could still play, unless that might make them biased.

- Have a couple of trial shots first, with no eliminations, so that everyone can get used to the rules.

- If you're shooting, it's really crucial that you're clear about whom you're shooting. Point with both arms, lock eyes with your target, and act it properly. If the person next to your target thinks they're being shot, too, it goes a bit wrong!

44. Co-Op Musical Islands

PLAYERS	DIFFICULTY	TIME
5-15	Easy	10 mins

IN SHORT: Much better than the original because you work together. This game works perfectly for any party, not just children's parties!

TAGS: COLLABORATIVE, ACTIVE, MUSIC

WHAT YOU'LL NEED

- An old newspaper, staples carefully removed (that's important!), then pulled apart into the big pages.

- A hi-fi or set of speakers to play your music.

HOW TO PLAY

Just like Pass the Present, Musical Chairs, or any other of these sorts of games, you'll want everybody standing up, with shoes and socks off, in a big space with nothing sharp around. The person playing and stopping the music might need a helper to remove islands, so aim to have at least two people to run the game.

The best thing about this game is that you have to work together to stay dry against the encroaching oceans, and so the frantic rush to get onto an island is a team effort, not a vicious, competitive one. Good team-building opportunities here.

Start by placing enough pieces of newspaper on the floor so that everyone will get their own island. Now play the music, and let everybody "swim" about the room. Swimming motions and general aquatic moves are encouraged, but not compulsory if you can't swim.

When the music stops, the sharks arrive. You could shout "QUICK! SHARKS!" as you stop the music. Everybody has about three seconds to "get to an island," which means standing on a piece of newspaper. Depending on the age and size of the group, you can give more or less time here, but the players need to get entirely clear of the "water" (the floor). If any part of them or their clothes is touching the carpet, they are gobbled up by sharks and eliminated.

Escaping the water is easy at first, but each time you start the music and everybody goes for a swim, the helpers should come and remove one of the pieces of newspaper. Then, when the music stops again, rather than players competing to be first to get to the newspaper, they will have to work together to share the shrinking islands. **The aim of the game is to save everyone.**

Once you get down to the nitty-gritty, and there are maybe four players for each sheet of newspaper, you could begin to remove little ribbons of paper from some of the pieces so that each one is a little smaller. Or, you could just go down to one piece, but with a team of fifteen swimmers this may be quite hard! At some point, people will begin to fall off into the sea. The winner, if you need one, would be the last person who hasn't been eaten by sharks, but the game must continue until absolutely everyone has been eliminated. It's funny to see the last person balancing a toe on a square inch of newspaper as the sharks surround them!

NOW TRY THIS

- If you want to make this game *truly* collaborative, then agree that the round ends as soon as *the first person* is eaten by sharks. That way, you must work together to save everyone for as long as possible, whether that means piggy-backs, crushed toes, or intense hugs.

45. Squashed Sardines

PLAYERS	DIFFICULTY	TIME
4-12	Easy	15 mins

IN SHORT: Hide-and-Seek to begin with, then a strange sort of shared hiding exercise. Great fun!

WHAT YOU'LL NEED

TAGS:
COLLABORATIVE,
ACTIVE, AROUND
THE HOUSE

• An apartment, house, or outdoor area in which to hide.

HOW TO PLAY

We all know how to play Hide-and-Seek. Everyone hides, one person seeks; if you get found, you become the seeker too until everyone's been found. The annoying thing about that game is that if you're *really* good at hiding, then the game might last forever. Once, at primary school, I eventually emerged from behind the garbage cans to find that my classmates had given up looking for me and started playing something else. One of the worst days of my life.

Well, **Squashed Sardines** suffers from none of the criticisms I could level at Hide-and-Seek.

One player is the hider. She gets as long as she needs (let's say three minutes) to find a good place to hide. Then, everybody else begins as the seeker. They must split up as well as they can for this game to work, so no teams of seekers. Why not have people setting off from the main room in intervals of thirty seconds?

But this is where the game is brilliant. If you find the hider, *you join them*. It will get harder and harder for you all to hide in whatever the chosen hiding place is, but that's the fun of it. As you cram together in the shower, try to stay silent and make sure nobody turns it on! Once you're all together again (which won't take long once the bodies pile up), set a new hider and begin the next round.

TIPS

- Before you start, count how many people are playing. You don't want to all be hiding under a duvet for hours before realizing that nobody else is looking for you and essentially you've gone for a collective nap.

- If the house you're playing in is too small, think where else this game could be played. The local park or other outdoor spaces might be fun, as long as you all know the game boundaries.

46. Who's the Leader?

PLAYERS	DIFFICULTY	TIME
5-20	Easy	5 mins per round

IN SHORT: Simple movement game where one player must figure out who is leading the actions.

WHAT YOU'LL NEED

TAGS: COLLABORATIVE, ACTIVE, CIRCLE GAMES

• Nothing at all.

HOW TO PLAY

Sit or stand in a circle. It works with either, but your choice depends on how active you plan on being!

One player leaves the room, while the others decide who will be the leader. This will change every round, so it doesn't matter who starts.

When the player returns, everyone else begins doing a repeated movement, such as patting their thighs or clicking their fingers. Every so often, maybe every ten seconds, the leader changes the movement, and all the other players have to change their movement as soon as they realize. At first, the changes in movement could be subtle and small, such as going from rubbing your arm to patting your arm to patting your shoulder.

The guesser can enter the circle or stay on the outside, moving about as much as she needs, but her goal is to work out who is the leader. She could look for eye contact, or for who seems to change their movements first. For this reason, all the players should stay aware of the leader's changes in movements as much as possible.

Once the guesser thinks she knows, she loudly announces the name of the leader. If she's right, she rejoins the circle and somebody else leaves the room for a new round. If she's wrong, the leader should start to make his changes of movements a bit more obvious. For example, if the guesser has guessed wrong three times, the leader might go straight from rubbing his tummy to clapping his hands. The sudden change and the new noise might give a good clue.

TIPS

- If you're the leader, try to vary the types of movements you do as much as possible. Think how each part of your body could make a unique repeated motion. There's twisting, bending, stretching, flicking, and wiggling, and that's just the tip of the hokey-cokey iceberg. Whatever changes you make, just try to make them when the guesser isn't looking.

- This may seem obvious, but if everyone just spends the game watching the leader to see when they change their movement, it's pretty easy for the guesser to follow their eyes. You need to be hiding whom you're watching so that you don't give the game away.

47. Chappy Tomato

PLAYERS	DIFFICULTY	TIME
5–15	Medium	20 mins

IN SHORT: Everybody chooses a silly name, then they must guess who's who while hoping that their own name isn't discovered.

TAGS: COMPETITIVE, MEMORY, CIRCLE GAMES

WHAT YOU'LL NEED

• Scraps of paper, equal-sized.

• Pens and paper for each player.

HOW TO PLAY

Sit in a circle and agree on one player to be the announcer. This will change each round.

The Setup

The announcer hands out slips of paper, and every other player must make up a silly name. What you write on the paper is entirely up to you, but it needs to be readable and possible to memorize. So, for example, "Sniffy Richard" or "Nelson Trout-Shoes" is fine, but "Mxctflsd" is impossible to read out loud, and "Adrian Philip 'Harrods' McCartney the Fifteenth of French Polynesia" is too long to remember. (Great name, though, if you're called that.) The announcer should not write a name, and should not compete in this round.

Once you've written your secret name, hand it to the announcer. The announcer checks to make sure they can all be read aloud. If not, it's not too late to ask the player to make another name!

When every player has given a name to the announcer, she shuffles them and then slowly reads out the names **TWICE**, making sure that nobody can see the slips of paper, in case they recognize handwriting. These are the only two times the players will officially hear the names, so listen carefully!

If the announcer reads your name wrong, **you must accept that your name is the one that the announcer reads**. It's probably your fault for having such terrible handwriting anyway.

The Main Game

The player on the announcer's left, Player 1, gets to ask the first question. She picks another player in the circle (not the announcer, though) and asks, "Player 2, are you _____?"

Player 2 must now respond. If Player 1 was correct, Player 2 must say, "Yes." She is now OUT and Player 1 gets another go. However, if Player 1 was wrong, or if he was right but said the name **significantly wrong**, then Player 2 says "No," and now it's Player 2's turn to guess. (Her name is "Sniffy Richard." So "Snotty Richard" or "Sniffing Richard" would be wrong. A mild pronunciation error is probably counted as correct.)

The last remaining unnamed player is the winner. She can jubilantly reveal her secret name to the group, and then becomes the announcer for the next round.

TIPS

- Often, as you approach the end, there are one or two names that everybody has forgotten. If this is your name, try to keep it secret for as long as possible. You could even guess a similar name, but wrong, to change people's memories of the real name. However, in some circles this is counted as cheating, or at least bad sportsmanship, so that's down to you.

- The hardest part of this game is memorizing the names. I use a simple form of **memory palace**, which is where you take a familiar journey (for me, it's walking through my parents' house) and mentally put the items you need to remember on that journey, interacting with each other.

48. Locked Box

PLAYERS	DIFFICULTY	TIME
2+	Medium	15 mins per round

IN SHORT: A guessing game where players must work out the rule for what fits in the box.

TAGS: STRATEGY, SPELLINGS, GUESSING, CIRCLE GAMES

WHAT YOU'LL NEED

• Nothing at all.

HOW TO PLAY

There is a locked box on one player's lap. Only she can look inside; for everybody else, the box is completely invisible!

Inside this box are all sorts of things, but they all follow one rule. The box-holder must decide **one rule** before the beginning of the round. For example, the items in the box could all:

• Have a meaningful link (all nature, all food, all one color, all made of metal, etc.).

• Begin with a particular letter.

• Be a word of a particular length.

• Rhyme with each other.

• Contain a double letter.

• Be said in a particular way (say "umm" beforehand or shrug as you say it, etc.).

• Be small enough to actually fit in the box.

• Not be in this room.

• Be worth $1,000 or more.

As you can see, the box-holder's rule could be anything. Be creative and make sure it isn't always about the meaning of the words. Think about the spelling, the sound, and everything else.

The box-holder begins by looking in the box and naming one thing that is inside. The other players now each get a chance to suggest another item that could be put in the box. If their word passes the rule, even if they don't know the rule, the box-holder says "Yes!" and takes the item. If their suggestion does not fit, the box-holder says "No."

Once every player has had a turn, the box-holder looks inside the box and names another thing inside. Other players should try to remember as many things that do fit inside the box as possible, in order to work out the rule.

The fun part about this game is that once other players know the rule, they don't reveal it. They just keep on guessing, following the rule so that every item they guess will fit inside the box! This, in turn, will make it easier for the others as they get more examples of things that fit.

Once everybody seems to know the rule and is getting every guess right, you can either discuss the rule or just move on to the next round. Make sure everybody gets a chance to hold the box and make up a rule.

TIPS

- There really is no limit to the rules that you could decide. Try things that relate to each player's own name, for example. You could make rules about how you're sitting, or how you move. At first, though, start simple.

- Try to never use the same rule twice. People will guess it really quickly!

49. Mafia

PLAYERS	DIFFICULTY	TIME
6–20	Medium	30 mins

IN SHORT: Root out the secret gangsters before they "kill" you in the night.

TAGS: COMPETITIVE, CONVERSATION, CIRCLE GAMES, STRATEGY

WHAT YOU'LL NEED

- Nothing at all.

HOW TO PLAY

This game is absolutely brilliant. It will need a large-ish group of players sitting around in a circle, so if you think you can organize that at a party, then do! It's probably not right for kids' parties, although I have regularly used this game with a full class of ten- and eleven-year-olds (and let me tell you, thirty players works but I don't recommend it).

You will need one player to be the host. They'll need to be pretty familiar with the rules, and confident enough to boss around a group for an extended period of time. (Whenever I play this game, I *love* being the host. It's such fun.)

It works like this. The host tells the assembled villagers that there are two Mafiosi in their midst. The aim of the game is to root them out and banish them from the village. Meanwhile, the aim of the Mafiosi is to "kill" all of the villagers, so that only they remain.

So, the first thing to happen is that everybody "goes to sleep" by closing and covering their eyes. Heads in laps is a good way to make sure nobody peeks. The host walks around the room, tapping two players on their shoulder. These are the two Mafiosi for this round. As quietly as possible, the Mafiosi must look up, identify each other, and go back to sleep. For the duration of the game, they must try to keep their identities secret by pretending to be villagers.

From now until the end of the game, we rotate between two periods:

Day

Every day, the assembled villagers (and Mafiosi, who are pretending to be villagers) must try to work out who among them are the Mafiosi. The host could prompt them with questions, or let the conversation naturally flow. Here are some open questions you could use to prompt conversation:

- Who in this circle can you definitely trust?

- Who would have wanted to kill **x** (the last eliminated player)?

- How do we know that you're a villager?

- Who do you think is a Mafioso?

It's quite good to follow accusations around the room. So, if Villager 1 accuses Villager 2, let Villager 1 explain why, and then give Villager 2 a chance to answer. Then ask her who she suspects, and so on.

After three to five minutes, the sun sets and it's time to banish someone. Everybody still alive, even the secret Mafiosi, votes for the person they think is a Mafioso, and the person with the most votes is banished. Before they leave the village to become a silent audience member, they must announce to the rest of the group whether they were a villager or a Mafioso.

Night

Immediately, everybody closes and covers their eyes, and once the host is sure nobody's peeking, the remaining Mafiosi uncover their eyes and decide, silently, whom they'll kill. Once they've made their target clear to the host, they go back to sleep, and the host announces that it's dawn and wakes everybody up. The host then reveals, with much drama, who has been murdered. That person is now a silent audience member. I like to go into gory details at this point, making up some horrible means of murder. This is optional.

The day begins again, but with fewer villagers. Just like yesterday, you spend the day discussing whom to banish. As the number of players decreases, things get tense and often rather exciting.

Ending the Game

The game can end in two ways:

- At the end of any day, if the villagers manage to vote out and banish the final Mafioso, they win. There should be much high-fiving and some sort of celebratory dance.

- At the beginning of a day, if the remaining Mafiosi have murdered enough people that only one villager remains, then at this point the remaining villager will immediately know who the Mafiosi are (I won't explain this, but just think about it). The game is essentially over. If there are two Mafiosi and one villager, then they have won. If there is one Mafioso and one villager, you could have a duel (see the section named "Duel" in the game **"Bang!"** on page 92 for more info on that).

NOW TRY THIS

- Once you become familiar with this game, there are various modifications you can add. It can get more and more complicated, but the new additions keep this game fresh for years. Why not try:

  1. **DETECTIVE:** A villager whom the host identifies as definitely innocent. She cannot be banished but can still be murdered.

  2. **MAYOR:** A villager who gets to banish an extra person at the end of every day. (You could even vote for a mayor at the beginning, but be careful of doing this. What if a Mafioso gets elected?)

  3. **DOCTOR:** A villager who may name one player per night who is protected from the Mafiosi's murdering grasp.

  4. **DUEL:** At any time, a player can challenge another to a duel. If the other player accepts, then follow the rules of a duel inside the game **"Bang!"** (see page 92). Last to say "Bang!" is dead, and their dying words will be to reveal if they were Mafioso or villager, before becoming a silent audience member.

- With different numbers of players, you can adapt the number of Mafiosi. With four villagers, having just one Mafioso can work. With thirty villagers, you might want three Mafiosi.

- In a similar vein, with more villagers, how about having more murders per night? I've gotten to a stage where each Mafioso gets to kill one person each night, just to speed things along.

TIPS

- One thing to be aware of is that it's very easy to cheat. If a player keeps his eyes secretly open at night, he'll see exactly who the Mafiosi are. So, the host should make it clear that cheaters on either side will be eliminated without warning, and keep a good watch on people who seem to have too much insight about what's going on!

- Also, once players are eliminated, they *must* remain silent. It's easy to want to remain involved in this game, but the host must make sure that once you're out, you're just a spectator.

- If you're the host, *think before you speak*. It's hard, but you have to treat the Mafiosi just like they're villagers, even when you know they aren't! I've accidentally given away a Mafioso just twice in my life, but both times it's ruined the game.

50. Pat Clap Click Click

PLAYERS	DIFFICULTY	TIME
3–15	Medium	10 mins per round

IN SHORT: A categories-naming game under pressure, in a circle, with movements.

TAGS: COMPETITIVE, RHYTHM, MEMORY, CIRCLE GAMES

WHAT YOU'LL NEED

• Nothing at all.

HOW TO PLAY

Sit in a circle and collectively agree on a category of things. It should be nice and broad to begin with, such as "Countries," "Films," or "Fruit and Vegetables," because the game is stressful enough without something difficult. However, as you feel more daring, or if you're among brainiacs, you could choose something a little more ambitious, such as "Ways to cook an egg" or "Adverbs." If you get stuck, I've included some ideas for categories on pages 251–52.

This game has a rhythm, which must be maintained, *or else!*

So, to begin with, settle into the rhythm as a group. It goes:

Pat—Clap—Click—Click—One—Two—Three—Four

The first four beats are movements: pat the table or your thighs, clap your hands, click the fingers of your left hand, click the fingers of your right hand. The next four beats you count in your head. Practice keeping those four beats absolutely silent, but still coming in together on *Pat*. It should be quite a challenge on its own, just to stay together and remember the order of the movements.

Now we introduce the categories. Each player takes turns naming something within that category, during the counting part of the rhythm. Essentially, they have four seconds to submit their answer, and then it's on to the next person.

At first, four seconds will feel like ages to submit an answer, but after a while it becomes quite tricky. No matter how quickly or slowly you answer, everybody else still counts to four in their heads before going back to *Pat*. The rhythm must continue, whatever happens.

If you don't answer in time, you're OUT, but the rhythm continues and it's on to the next person. For this reason, unless you don't mind the game stopping every time someone gets it wrong, it's self-policing. If you miss an answer, back away from the circle and let the others continue. You'll get a chance to come back in for the next round.

TIP

- The temptation is to speed up early on, or not to count to four in your head and come in with the next *Pat* as soon as the player has said their word. Don't do it! The rhythm keeps the game going and soon becomes a really satisfying way of imposing a time limit when the answers get harder.

NOW TRY THIS

- If you're familiar with the song "Cup" from the film *Pitch Perfect*, you'll know there are places you can go with this game. I recommend searching out that particular song, learning the skill (I'd say it's tied for my top party trick, along with breathing out of my eye) and playing this same game, but saying your word on the last cup-slam of that famous rhythm.

CHAPTER 6
CABIN FEVER

It's a Sunday afternoon in early February. The rain snivels down like a nose with a persistent cold. You wouldn't leave the house even if it were on fire, yet there's nothing to do inside either. You're so bored that the word "bored" has become boring. The kids are climbing the walls (not literally). Hang on, yes, literally. Your five-year-old is now hanging from the curtain.

You need something, *anything* to entertain you before headaches, crying, and comfort food absorb your entire weekend. And guess what I have in this chapter?

I've collected these games with a rainy weekend in mind. Some use your home for inspiration, so there's no reason to leave it, but you'll be using it in a very different way from usual. Others are creative or absorbing enough to have you ignoring Storm Desmond, or whatever they're calling him, and whiling away the afternoon until it turns into evening. You're just one scrap of paper or, in one case, a saucepan away from a perfectly pleasant day together, even though you're stuck inside.

51. Sniffer Dog

PLAYERS	DIFFICULTY	TIME
2+	Easy	5 mins per round

IN SHORT: One player draws an item that's nearby. Everybody else has to go and find it.

TAGS: ARTSY, MEMORY, AROUND THE HOUSE, ACTIVE

WHAT YOU'LL NEED

- A pad of paper (you'll be drawing all around the house, not always on a table) and a pencil.

- A place where you can safely move around without disturbing people or their belongings.

HOW TO PLAY

The game begins with all players exploring the surrounding area, carefully taking mental note of everything they can see. The players decide on a certain area as their "boundary"—for example, the house, but not outside it.

Now, one player, the artist, chooses something in the area that's easily visible (i.e., not hidden in a box or behind a locked door) and draws a picture of it on a piece of paper. The other players are the sniffer dogs. At any point during the drawing, the sniffer dogs may peel off to find that item. When they think they've found it, they bark loudly and place their hand or finger on the item, at which point everybody else comes to see. If they're correct, they win the round and it's their turn to draw. If not, the artist continues to draw their item until it is found.

No sniffer dog may bark, woof, or whine **unless they have their paw on the item**. If they bark as they're searching, then it sends a dishonest message to the other players, so they're in the doghouse (sitting out) for the rest of that round. If two sniffer dogs are barking at the same time, the artist should know the location where the real item actually is, and so be able to discern who is the winning dog.

If two sniffer dogs find the item at the same time, the round is a tie and they can decide between them who draws next round.

52. Endless Sentence

PLAYERS	DIFFICULTY	TIME
2	Easy	15 mins

IN SHORT: One player tells a story. The other makes sure that their sentence never ends.

TAGS: GRAMMAR, CREATIVE, STORYTELLING, COLLABORATIVE

WHAT YOU'LL NEED

• Nothing at all.

HOW TO PLAY

First of all, you need to be acquainted with conjunctions. These words, also known as connectives or "joiny bits," according to one of my pupils, are the glue that stick two clauses together. (A clause is a group of words that makes sense on its own.) So, for example, "The dog bit the postman **because** he looked so tasty."

Without conjunctions, your sentences can contain only one clause, and that's just boring! Below is a cloud of conjunctions. You'll need to keep this page open, probably, when you play the game. If you can't hold the page open, then spell out the words in shaving cream or tattoo them on your grandmother's arm. Not literally, of course, unless she's down for that sort of thing.

Conjunctions Cloud

• additionally	• as long as	• by the time
• afterward	• as soon as	• consequently
• also	• as well as	• despite the fact that
• although	• because	• due to
• and	• before	• even though
• as if	• but	• for

- furthermore
- however
- in case
- including
- meanwhile
- moreover
- nevertheless
- next
- once

- or
- or else
- otherwise
- owing to
- since
- so
- so that
- then
- though

- unless
- until
- when
- whenever
- where
- wherever
- while
- yet

To play this game, the storyteller will begin a story with a simple sentence. You can use a first line from my list (see page 246) or come up with your own. The only limitation is that it must be a whole clause (containing a subject and an action) and not just a short phrase. "Once upon a time," for example, is not enough, because "Once upon a time **and** . . ." doesn't make sense.

Then the other player, the conjoiner, will shout out one of the conjunctions from the cloud, and the storyteller must continue the story using that conjunction. The twist is that at the end of every clause, the conjoiner will shout another conjunction, so that your sentence goes on and on, telling the whole story without ever stopping. It's amazing how far your story can go on one sentence.

Once the story has reached a natural end, you can stop shouting conjunctions and the roles will swap. Now it's the other player's turn to try the Endless Sentence.

EXAMPLE

Storyteller: *"Timmy the seal went for a swim . . ."*
Conjoiner: *"after . . ."*
Storyteller: *"he'd finished his dinner . . ."*
Conjoiner: *"because . . ."*

Storyteller: *"he felt fat and flabby . . ."*
Conjoiner: *"so . . ."*
Storyteller: *"he swam far out into the ocean . . ."*
Conjoiner: *"where . . ."*
Storyteller: *"he found a grumpy whale, filtering plankton . . ."*
Etc.

TIPS

- If you are the conjoiner, you must listen carefully to the story and be as involved as the storyteller. Not all conjunctions will work at the end of every clause. If I say "One day, I climbed a mountain" and you add "or else," I'm stuck.

- You could try to use every conjunction on the list, or repeat the same one again and again. Try a mixture!

53. Pan Tapping

PLAYERS	DIFFICULTY	TIME
2+	Easy	5 mins

IN SHORT: Help a player find an item just by tapping.

WHAT YOU'LL NEED

TAGS: ACTIVE, GUESSING, RHYTHM, AROUND THE HOUSE

- Something you can tap on. Tambourines, wooden spoons on saucepans, or just use your voice.

HOW TO PLAY

Have one player, the hunter, leave the room. The other players should decide between them on **an item** in the room (or the whole house, if you like) that you want the hunter to find.

The hunter now reenters the room and the rest of the players begin to tap their pans in a slow and steady rhythm, like a drumbeat. If you have nothing to tap, use your voice. Start with a low hum.

The closer the hunter gets to the item, the faster you tap your pan, or the higher you hum. If they move away again, you tap slower again. Just by listening to your taps, they can track down the exact location of the hidden item. Make sure you don't look at the item!

When the hunter touches the item, they win! It's time to choose another player to leave the room.

NOW TRY THIS

This game can also be played by choosing a particular movement or gesture rather than an item. You tap your pan faster the closer the hunter gets to making that movement. For example, if you want the hunter to get on their hands and knees and bark like a dog, then you would tap faster when they lean over, then faster still when they kneel, etc. . . .

54. Silly Word Snowballs

PLAYERS	DIFFICULTY	TIME
2+	**Easy**	**15 mins**

IN SHORT: Create special snowballs containing words to make your opponents laugh.

TAGS: ACTIVE, AROUND THE HOUSE, SILLY

WHAT YOU'LL NEED

- Permission from the person who owns the house that it's okay to throw paper around—make sure there's nothing breakable nearby.

- Pencils and scrap paper. (Don't use nice paper for this. You'll use a lot.)

HOW TO PLAY

First of all, you need to make some silly snowballs. To do this, write a short sentence or just a word on a piece of paper, and then scrunch it up. It doesn't even need to be a real word—whatever you think will make the other players laugh.

To begin with, why not make about **three** snowballs each.

When you're ready, the snowball fight begins. Count down from ten together so that you can all get to a shielded space, and on zero, begin!

As soon as a paper snowball directly hits another player, everybody who sees it shouts "CEASEFIRE!" and the round ends. (Picking up a snowball does not count as it "hitting" you.)

At this point, the person who was hit by a snowball must stand up straight, pick up the snowball that hit her, and unscrunch it. She must then read aloud the contents of that snowball without laughing. If you want to be mean, you could decide beforehand that she cannot even smile.

If she laughs (or smiles), then the person who wrote the snowball gets a point. If not, then she gets a point. If she wrote the snowball that hit her, she must scrunch that one up without reading it aloud and pick up the nearest one to her.

The "used" snowball is cast aside (in the recycling) and after a countdown, the game begins again. If you're low on snowballs, then between rounds you should make some more.

The game ends when it actually begins to snow and you can all go outside to play the real version of this game.

TIPS

- Think about the things that will make somebody laugh when forced to say them out loud. There are plenty of great gags that are amusing when delivered right, but a different sort of thing will make me chuckle as I read it.

- There's no rule as to what the other players can do while the hit player is reading out their snowball, but a tense silence is often the most conducive to making them laugh. There is such a thing as trying too hard to be funny.

55. The Floor Is Lava

PLAYERS	DIFFICULTY	TIME
2+	Easy	Endless

IN SHORT: A great physical game to play at home.
Just don't play it around precious things.

TAGS:
ACTIVE,
AROUND THE
HOUSE, SILLY

WHAT YOU'LL NEED

• Permission from the person who owns the house
  that it's okay to climb on their furniture.

HOW TO PLAY

This is an ongoing game, which works best when sprung upon people in the
room/area at random times. Simply, one person yells "The floor is lava!" and
then starts counting down from five. Every other person must be completely
off the ground by the time the counter reaches zero. What, or whom, they
climb on is up to them, but if any part of them remains on the ground, then
they'll be burnt to a crisp.

NOW TRY THIS

• At this point, you've probably had enough fun and someone might have
  broken a vase or an ankle, but you're likely wondering when you're
  allowed to get down. The game can continue if you challenge other
  players to reach a certain place without touching the ground. Watch as
  each player creatively devises a plan for crossing the dangerous lava
  without burning their toes.

56. The Silent Game

PLAYERS	DIFFICULTY	TIME
2+	Easy	Depends how good you are!

IN SHORT: Shh!

WHAT YOU'LL NEED

- Nothing at all.

TAGS:
COMPETITIVE,
AROUND THE
HOUSE, SILLY

HOW TO PLAY

Glorious! A game that gets people to be quiet! Well . . . it isn't that simple, because the aim of the game is to get your opponents to make a noise. You could do anything, be that making silly faces, giving an intense stare, or pretending to be a gorilla.

Any noise counts, so listen for footsteps, sighing, or the odd occasional snort.

The thing is, not being able to make a noise makes everything more tense. If you're looking to quiet some people down, look in the Just Chill Out chapter (page 207). This one's all about self-awareness and poise . . . not exactly a relaxing experience.

An important rule here is that there should be **no physical contact**. Of course your opponent will make some noise if you hit them hard enough. Where's the fun in that?

NOW TRY THIS

- How about both trying to do a normal life task without making a noise? You could try pairing socks, cooking dinner together, or taking the kids to school, all without making a single noise. I wonder how it'll change your appreciation of the little things . . .

57. Disregarded Things

PLAYERS	DIFFICULTY	TIME
2+	Medium	10–20 mins

IN SHORT: Adopt the personality of forgotten things in your house, and see how long the other players take to find them.

TAGS: CREATIVE, GUESSING, AROUND THE HOUSE

WHAT YOU'LL NEED

- Nothing at all.

HOW TO PLAY

I found this game years ago in one of Pie Corbett's excellent books on literacy, *Jumpstart! Literacy*, and had to include a version of it. It was originally devised by the poet Philip Gross, and I think it's genius.

Move around a room and try to find something that you think nobody else will have seen. It might be a scrap of paper on the floor or a shoe mark on the baseboard.

Now try to imagine you *are* that thing. Tell the other players what it feels like to be you, what you can see from where you are, how you came to be where you are, what it's like living wherever you live. Don't give too many obvious clues about where you're found, but make sure that you're really in the character of your disregarded thing.

The other players must search the room, trying to work out who you are. Eventually they'll find you, and somebody else will play the role of their disregarded thing.

TIP

- This game is all about personification, which takes empathy. Bringing an item to life is all about trying to imagine what they'd feel, say, think, and do if they were alive. It's not easy, which is all the more reason to try it.

58. Monsters of the Nook and Cranny

PLAYERS	DIFFICULTY	TIME
1+	Medium	It entirely depends

IN SHORT: Your house is full of tiny monsters. Or, at least, it will be after you've finished this game.

TAGS: CREATIVE, ARTSY, AROUND THE HOUSE, LONG-TERM

WHAT YOU'LL NEED

- Modeling material (clay, plasticine, cold porcelain, etc.) OR drawing equipment.

HOW TO PLAY

Explore your house as if you're looking for mice, or other tiny beasts. Think of all the places they might live: In the kitchen cupboards? In the pocket of an old coat? At the bottom of the toothbrush holder?

In this game, you will imagine what tiny, evil (or cute) monsters live in these little unexplored places, then create those monsters and leave them there, never to be found. (Eventually, they *will* be found, and that's the joy of this game. How long will they hide before somebody comes across them?)

So, once you've decided on your hidden nook or cranny in your house, imagine what sort of beast would make it their home. What would the monster do down there? What would it eat? What would make that little space the perfect home for your monster?

Have a go at drawing your monster, giving it a name, and writing down what it spends its day doing.

Next, it's time to create your monster. If you have some modeling clay or plasticine, use this. Make it as small as it needs to be. Think about which animal or monster parts it will have. (Legs or wings? Antennae? A shell?) What color would it need to be to blend in with its environment, never to be found?

If you don't have any modeling materials, draw your monster on a tiny square of paper or card.

Once your model/drawing is finished, it is time to deliver him to his new home. Make sure he's safe in there. If you like, you could leave a little message of explanation. It could say who this monster is, why he is where he is, and what anyone should do if they find him.

Leave your monster to his new life. If you like, check on him after a few days to see if he's settled in. The more monsters you can create and hide away in your house, the better you are doing at this game!

IMPORTANT

- If you have little children or animals who roam about the house, don't leave anything small and swallowable anywhere that they could get their tiny mitts or paws on. If you're playing this game on your own, it might be worth checking with one other person that this is a good place to hide your monster.

59. Jumble

PLAYERS	DIFFICULTY	TIME
1+	Medium	5 mins per round

IN SHORT: A well-known anagrams game.

WHAT YOU'LL NEED

TAGS:
SPELLING,
VOCABULARY,
COMPETITIVE

- Letter cards (see below), cut up and put in two separate hats.

- A mini whiteboard and one dry-erase marker per player, or paper and pencils.

- Timer—use a stopwatch or your phone.

- Dictionary (online is fine) to check spellings.

HOW TO PLAY

As you can see, there's a little preparation needed for this game. It won't take long, and don't be put off, as it's well worth the effort.

Cut some paper or card into little squares. On each one you'll need to write a letter, but it's quite important you get the number of each letter right.

Vowels: You need 4 of **E**, 3 of **A**, 3 of **I**, 3 of **O**, and 1 of **U**. Put these 14 cards in the vowels hat.

Consonants: You need 5 each of **D**, **L**, **N**, **R**, **S**, and **T**, 3 each of **C**, **G**, **M**, and **P**, and 1 each of **B**, **F**, **H**, **J**, **K**, **Q**, **V**, **W**, **X**, **Y**, and **Z**. Put these 53 cards in the consonants hat.

Each round, one player will select nine letters from the hats and place them on the table. You can select however many vowels and consonants you like, but you must pick the cards one by one and not look inside the hats as you pick. A mixture of vowels and consonants is useful, but you'll soon learn how many of each is best, and even if you get it wrong, at least everyone will have the same challenge.

Once the cards have been picked, put one minute on the timer and begin.

The aim is to spell the longest word using the letters that you have chosen. If playing alone, you can jumble around the cards to find your word.

You may not use proper nouns (names such as "London," "Facebook," or "John"), slang ("Haha," "Gotcha"), or abbreviations ("BRB," "LOL").

At the end of the time, the players share the longest word they have found. I like to give everybody points equal to their longest word. Alternatively, this game works perfectly well without scoring whatsoever.

EXAMPLE

The letters chosen are: A G P D E I T S P.

Player 1's *longest word is "TIPS." She gets 4 points.*

Player 2's *longest word is "PEPSI," but that is a proper noun. His next-longest word is "AGES." He gets 4 points.*

Player 3's *longest word is "DESPITE," which would give 7 points, but she used E twice. Her second-best word, "PAGES," earns her 5 points.*

TIPS

- After each round, why not use an online resource such as www .thewordfinder.com to find the longest possible word? Some of the top ones are just impossible to get, but see if there was a word longer than yours that you could have found. Which blends of consonants did it use? How did the word begin and end? These sorts of questions will help you develop some skills for the next round.

- Try looking for common word endings such as "ING" and "ED."

- If you are getting only three- to four-letter words, try blending the consonants on offer. "ND" often go together in a word, as do "ST." Play around with these blends instead of single letters.

NOW TRY THIS

- Collect everyone's longest (or favorite) word from the same round and put them together into a stupid sentence. So, in this round, the sentence could be "It takes me **ages** to write any **pages** of this book because the **tips** on my pens keep breaking."

60. Double Acrostic

PLAYERS	DIFFICULTY	TIME
1+	Medium	10 mins

IN SHORT: One acrostic on the left, one on the right, your words in the middle. Can you do it?

WHAT YOU'LL NEED

TAGS: WIND-DOWN, VOCABULARY, SPELLING

• Paper and pencils.

HOW TO PLAY

This game is calming and satisfying: perfect for long days indoors.

An acrostic is a word game or poem where certain letters of each line form a word. In this case we will end up with several words listed on a page, for which the first and last letters will form words reading upward and downward.

Think of **two** words that have the **same number of letters**. They could be names, two related places, or anything, really. Write one word vertically downward on the left of your page, and the other going upward on the right-hand side of the page.

Your job is to find words that begin with the letter on the left and end with the letter on the right. It doesn't matter how long or short the connecting word is. Write them in to join the two words.

EXAMPLE

I've made a double acrostic with two of my favorite words: "chocolate milkshake." One goes down on the left, one goes up on the right.

```
C        A    K                      E
H        A    D    D    O    C        K
O        M    E    G                  A
C        R    A    S                  H
O    L   I    V    E                  S
L    I   M    E    R    I    C        K
A    S   T    R    A                  L
T    A   N    D    O    O    R        I
E    D   A                           M
```

NOW TRY THIS

- If you want your double acrostic to remain a smart, juicy grid, then why not try to find words of the same length to fit each row? It's a tough challenge, so perhaps wait to decide how long every word must be until you've got a few ideas.

CHAPTER 7

LONG GAMES FOR LONG JOURNEYS

Uncle Brian and his family of seven have driven down from Buffalo for a Sunday at your home. The house is a mess: you meant to tidy it during the week, but each evening felt like its own episode of *Fawlty Towers*. You've stuck all the clutter in a couple of rooms and firmly closed the doors, and put the really nice fruit bowl from your trip to Morocco on the kitchen table to distract from the pile of unopened letters and half-read newspapers next to it.

Now they've arrived, all of them, including a puppy so massive that "puppy" is false advertising, and your house suddenly feels sardine-can cramped. You try to make tea, but the kettle needs boiling three times just to fill eleven mugs. Within minutes, the kids have found your messy rooms and the really nice fruit bowl from your trip to Morocco has been tail-wagged off the kitchen table.

You hear the words coming out of your mouth before you realize you're about to say them: "Let's go for a walk."

Now you're a quarter of a mile from home and starting to regret it. You forgot your gloves, the dog has caught a pigeon, the girls are so bored that they're singing a song about it, and you still have nothing to say to Uncle Brian. Luckily, here are ten games for this very situation.

These are the sorts of games that liven up long periods of time when all you can do is chat. They're conversation starters, talking duels, guessing games, and creative challenges. Once you've got started on these, you'll want your long walk to be five miles longer, your train journey to last three more stations, or your bus to get rerouted.

61. The Questions Game

PLAYERS	DIFFICULTY	TIME
2	Easy	10 mins

IN SHORT: Answer questions with questions for as long as you can in this head-to-head battle.

WHAT YOU'LL NEED

- Nothing at all.

HOW TO PLAY

One player begins by asking the other a question. It could be anything, but here are a couple of suggested starters:

- What's the time?

- What's your favorite food?

- What do you want to do today?

- When did you last have a bath?

The second player must respond with a relevant question to continue the conversation, rather than an answer. Don't just respond "Could you repeat that?" or "What?"

The whole conversation must be made of questions. You aren't allowed to repeat any questions, either. The first person to make a statement or command loses.

EXAMPLE

Player 1: "What's for dinner?"
Player 2: "What makes you think I'm cooking?"
Player 1: "Who else would cook dinner?"
Player 2: "Couldn't you do it?"

Player 1: *"Have you seen me try to cook?"*

Player 2: *"When are you going to learn?"*

Player 1: *"I don't know. When are you going to teach me?"*

Player 1 loses because *"I don't know"* is not a question but a statement.

TIPS

- Open questions are always better than closed ones. So, start your sentences with one of the five Ws (what, who, where, why, when) over a word like "did" or "is," which provoke only a yes-or-no answer.

- If in doubt, turn your opponent's question around on them.

- Watch out for little statements before your question, like "No" or "I don't know." They're often the way people end up losing!

62. Buzz Words

PLAYERS	DIFFICULTY	TIME
2+	Easy	5 mins per round

IN SHORT: Avoid the electric shocks by guessing words that don't contain the buzz letter.

TAGS:
CODE,
GUESSING,
SPELLING

WHAT YOU'LL NEED

- Nothing at all.

HOW TO PLAY

This is a little bit like the spelling version of **Locked Box** (see page 102).

One player, the buzzer, chooses a "buzz letter"—a letter that must not be contained in any words, or you'll get an electric shock. The buzzer must keep this letter a secret, if they know what's good for them.

The guessers must take turns saying a word. If the buzz letter is in their word, then the buzzer can call, "Buzz!" If you're really good friends, then this could be accompanied by a tickle, but you absolutely have to agree on this before you start the game. I hate being tickled with such a passion that if you did it to me I'd immediately stop talking to you.

As you go, try to find the letter that has caused the buzz. Soon, you'll be avoiding buzzes at every turn, to the annoyance of the buzzer.

Once everybody has avoided buzzes for a few rounds, switch roles and let somebody else choose the buzz letter.

EXAMPLE

Buzzer *has chosen "g" as his buzz letter.*
Guesser 1: *"Norway."*
Buzzer *says nothing.*
Guesser 2: *"Sausage."*
Buzzer: *"Buzz!"*
Guesser 1 *thinks the buzz letter might be "s," so tests it out. "Sarcastic."*

Buzzer *says nothing, so Guesser 1 knows it isn't "s."*
Guesser 2 tries a similar word. "Savage."
Buzzer: *"Buzz!"*
Guesser 1: "Sage."
Buzzer: *"Buzz!"*
Guesser 2 thinks the buzz letter might be g, so begins to avoid it. "Sauce."
Buzzer *says nothing.*
Guesser 1 thinks he has it too, but once again tests it. "Egg."
Buzzer: *"Buzz!"*
Etc.

TIPS

- Hold the letters from each buzz word in your head, so that next time there's a buzz word, you can see which letters are in both. Soon you'll have your answer, and no more electric shocks.

- There will be times when players accidentally avoid buzzes for ages, just because they aren't guessing the right (or wrong) letters. It'll be pretty obvious when they know the letter, though.

NOW TRY THIS

- You can play this game with a whiteboard if it's too hard in your head, or if you just really like whiteboards. Write down your guess, and make two lists—"Letters that I can use" and "Letters that I might not be able to use." Soon you'll find the answer, when the second list has one item.

- If you want this game to last for ages, keep the buzz letter going, even after everyone knows what it is. If anybody uses that letter in conversation, then "Buzz!"

63. Glom!

PLAYERS	DIFFICULTY	TIME
2+	**Easy**	**10 mins**

IN SHORT: A quick-fire game where players win by talking nonsense.

TAGS:
VOCABULARY,
SILLY,
CONVERSATION,
COMPETITIVE

WHAT YOU'LL NEED

- Nothing at all.

HOW TO PLAY

This game is total nonsense. It works like this: take turns blurting out a nonsense word. This is quick-fire. No time to think or craft your word, and no repetitions. Your word must be one syllable long, not two or more. Have a look at **Avagat** (see page 62) for more information on identifying syllables.

Here's the catch. With one-syllable words, it is surprisingly easy to accidentally say a real word. If you do, your opponent gets a point. If you pause for too long, your opponent gets a point. If you repeat a word, your opponent gets a point. If your word has more than one syllable, your opponent gets a point. First to one million points wins.

One more thing: you might hit a rich seam of nonsense words by finding a funny ending and changing the first consonant: "Totch, Fotch, Yotch, Spotch," and so on. For that reason, you aren't allowed to say two words in a row that rhyme. Make each word sound different or it's both naughty and cheating.

EXAMPLE

Player 1: "Spooch."
Player 2: "Ling."
Player 1: "Crab. Oh no!"
Player 2: "That's a word. I get a point. Right, I'll start again: clug."
Player 1: "Tresh."

Player 2: *(slowly)* *"F . . . .oo . . . j?"*
Player 1: *"Too slow! I get a point."*

TIPS

- Think of the spelling of words in your head as you're saying them. Remember, most one-syllable words go consonant-vowel-consonant. Look for odd combinations and hope they don't make real words!

- In the end, though, it's not about how you spell the word inside your head. It's about how it sounds. You may have spelled the word "kasshe" but it sounds like "cash," so your opponent gets a point.

64. Yes/No/Black/White

PLAYERS	DIFFICULTY	TIME
2+	Hard	Ongoing

IN SHORT: Try to trick a player into saying one of the four words in this game's title.

TAGS: STRATEGY, CONVERSATION, SILLY, COMPETITIVE

WHAT YOU'LL NEED

• Nothing at all.

HOW TO PLAY

Yes, no, black, and white. Four little words. Hard to forget them, really. So why is this game so difficult?

The rules of the game are simple. One player, the responder, has to attempt to **avoid** saying the words "Yes," "No," "Black," or "White" for as long as possible, while being asked a barrage of questions by the other players. As soon as she says one of the forbidden words, she is OUT and someone else takes a turn as the responder.

The responder may not ignore any questions. She must answer every single one with an answer that makes sense.

The responder is also not allowed to nod or shake her head. This works well because, if I may speak for myself, I have no idea what I'm doing with my head most of the time. You could extend this rule to any sounds such as "mm-hmm" and "uh-uh," which clearly mean yes and no. Similarly, choose right now whether or not to ban words like "yeah" and "nah."

EXAMPLE

Questioner: "What's your favorite color?"
Responder: "Red."
Questioner: "Really?"
Responder: "Yeah . . . oh bother."

TIP

- If the responder is really good, try to distract them by asking difficult questions that take a lot of explanation, or even asking questions that *don't* require the four words to answer, to catch them off guard. For example, you could ask, "When was the last time you've been to France?" Let them talk, and then follow it up with "And have you ever been to Italy?" They won't see it coming.

NOW TRY THIS

There are a number of variant rules that people choose to add. You could try them and see if they make it harder or easier.

- You may not repeat the answer to a question. This plays around those players who just answer "Dunno" to everything.

- *Fun version alert!* If you don't like fun, don't read on . . . okay. Here we go. Everybody is both questioner and responder at the same time. Ask a question to your opponent, trying to get them to say one of the four words, without saying the words yourself. If you say it, you sit out the rest of the round and see who's left at the end. Tough, but great.

65. Adjectival Animals

PLAYERS	DIFFICULTY	TIME
2+	Hard	Ongoing

IN SHORT: A to-and-fro game that will have you cackling from the wonderfully silly images it conjures.

TAGS:
GRAMMAR,
VOCABULARY,
CREATIVE

WHAT YOU'LL NEED

- Nothing at all.

HOW TO PLAY

Take turns coming up with **an animal** and **an adjective** to describe that animal. The only twist is that both words MUST begin with the **same letter**. This is called alliteration, and it's nice.

Try to get a really good flow by allowing only a second or two to think. You can either go through the alphabet, like in an **"A–Z of . . . ,"** or just jump around as you like.

If you want to be competitive, if anybody gets stuck or doesn't use alliteration, then they are OUT for the rest of the round. If you don't want that, just keep on playing. As usual, the sillier the better.

EXAMPLE

Player 1: "Moronic monkey."
Player 2: "Lazy lizard."
Player 3: "Iconic iguana."
Player 1: "Sausage snake."
Player 3: "Sausage isn't a describing word!"
Player 1: "All right, sarcastic snake."
Etc.

TIPS

- Some people find it easier to think of the animal first, and some think of the adjective. Try both and see which works for you!

- If you're trying for a complete adjectival animal alphabet run, good luck on N, Q, U, and X. If you really need help and you can't use the Internet, see below.*

NOW TRY THIS

- This leads into some excellent creative writing opportunities. Use your favorite adjectival animals and expand them into sentences containing bags of alliteration. So, "Grumpy Gorilla" is all well and good, but how about turning it into: "The grumpy gorilla gloriously grinned after gulping down a green grape." Notice that not every word has to start with G, but most do.

---

* Newt, Narwhal, Quetzal, Quagga, Unicorn (!!!), Upupa, Xerus, X-ray fish. And yes, of course I looked up most of those. I bet you couldn't identify a xerus if you saw one in the post office.

66. Similelarly

PLAYERS	DIFFICULTY	TIME
2	Medium	15 mins

IN SHORT: A cooperative ideas game that creates strange similes.

TAGS: CREATIVE, PUNS, GRAMMAR, CONVERSATION

WHAT YOU'LL NEED

- Pencil and paper to record your results, if you want.

HOW TO PLAY

This is a slow game, so you'll need to be comfortable with pauses, silences, and giving each other time to think. That said, it's brilliant, so give it a chance.

Let's start with what a simile is. It's when you bring in a new image by saying something is *like* or *as* something else:

- Rain drizzled down like a leaking pipe.
- This curry is as hot as the sun!
- My drive to work was like a film: long, full of twists and turns, and I fell asleep toward the end.

They're very useful when you're trying to describe to the reader/listener something they *don't* know, by likening it to something they *do* know.

This game comes in two levels. I recommend warming up with Level 1, then, once you're confident, moving on to the more entertaining but slightly harder Level 2.

LEVEL 1

It works a little like **Word Association** (see page 208). One player states a random thing, person, or action. Now the second player must think of another thing, person, or action that is linked to the first one in some way, and give a reason. He will give his answer in the format: "_____ *is like* _____: *they both* _____."

Now the first player will have to think of a new thing, person, or action that is like the previous object and link them together somehow, and so on. The best part is that you can link objects in simple ways (*"They both have wheels"*) or in complicated ways (*"They both give you bad breath," "They'd both make bad birthday presents," "They both whistle"*). The aim of the game is to make the longest chain of similes possible. Here's an example.

EXAMPLE (LEVEL 1)

Player 1: *"A ball."*
Player 2: *"A ball is like an orange: they are both perfectly round."*
Player 1: *"An orange is like a rhinoceros: they both have tough skin."*
Player 2: *"A rhinoceros is like a battleship: they are both gray."*
Player 1: *"A battleship is like a rubber duck: they both float on water."*
Player 2: *"A rubber duck is like a guinea pig: they both squeak when you squeeze them."*
Etc.

LEVEL 2

Once you've mastered Level 1, you may choose to move on. Here's where the game becomes a little more complex, but a step more fun.

Play the game just as before, still thinking of a new item that is similar in some way to the old one, but this time, don't say the reason for your simile out loud. It is the other player's job to work out the link. They will think about it, then say the reason for you.

It doesn't matter if they get the same reason as you. In fact, it's just as much fun to find different reasons why the two things are linked as it is to find the same one.

EXAMPLE (LEVEL 2)

Player 1: "A lion."

Player 2: " . . . is like a motorbike."

Player 1: "Because they make growling noises?"

Player 2: "Ooh, that's good! I was thinking about their speed. Your turn."

Player 1: "A motorbike is like a deep fryer."

Player 2: "You fill it with oil?"

Player 1: "Yes!"

Player 2: "A deep fryer is like a swimming pool."

Etc.

NOW TRY THIS

- If you want a really challenging version, then count down from three together and both say random words at the same time. Then it's your job to think of a simile that relates the two. Be patient: this game is difficult!

67. Celebritables

PLAYERS	DIFFICULTY	TIME
2+	**Hard**	**15 mins +**

IN SHORT: Pass the hours by turning celebrities into vegetables.

TAGS:
COLLABORATIVE,
PUNS,
WIND-DOWN

WHAT YOU'LL NEED

• If a good idea strikes you, then drawing materials.

• For the rest of us: nothing at all.

HOW TO PLAY

A great game to play as you wander along, zoning in and out as you let your mind wander.

Combine the name of a **celebrity** with the name of a **vegetable** (or a fruit, I guess) to create a quaint yet surprising image.

You can make a pun from their first name, for example, Broccoli Obama, or their surname, like Donald Trumpkin.

After each suggestion, it's illuminating to discuss how the celebrity and the vegetable are mingled. Perhaps Chilli Chaplin has a spicy mustache and suit over his shiny red skin, while Okra Winfrey's a slightly slimy but charismatic TV host. You could discuss how their careers would have been different if they contained seeds, or had peelable skin. Finally, you could suggest the most delicious way to cook them.

NOW TRY THIS

• You know what's better than imagining these vegetebrities? Drawing them. Send me your best ones via Twitter @IvanBrett, because I want to create a gallery of these but can't draw to save my life.

• If you want a few more categories to try out, how about "Baking Musicians" (Scone Lennon, James Brownie) or "Movies About Animals" (*Manchester by the Seagull, Honey I Skunk the Kids*)?

68. Essence

PLAYERS	DIFFICULTY	TIME
2+	**Hard**	**Ongoing**

IN SHORT: Discover the identity of a person by asking about their "essence."

TAGS:
WIND-DOWN,
COLLABORATIVE,
CONVERSATION,
CREATIVE

WHAT YOU'LL NEED

- Nothing at all.

HOW TO PLAY

One player, the leader, thinks of somebody whom everyone else in the car knows: a family member, friend, or colleague. It works best if you don't use celebrities because there are far too many of them and—sorry to break it to you—you don't know what they're really like, only what they want you to think they're like.

The leader keeps that person in their head, while the guessers take turns asking questions to work out whom they're thinking about. Here's the catch, though: they may ask only metaphorical questions that inquire about the character's *essence*. For example:

- What animal are they?
- What item of clothing are they?
- What color are they?
- What shop are they?
- What city are they?
- What plant are they?
- What TV show are they?
- What game are they?
- What vehicle are they?
- What decade are they?
- What noise are they?
- What flavor are they?

The leader must not take the questions too literally. Yes, this person is human, but that isn't the answer to the first question. Perhaps this person is a dog, because they are loyal, or maybe they're a monkey, because they're cheeky. Whatever the case, you should answer with just one word. "Leopard," for example.

The guessers may not ask any question that actually provides information that would help identify the character. So, for example, questions like "What gender are they?" or "What age are they?" are banned. This game is completed only with essences and metaphors, not real facts.

Once they think they know, a guesser can guess the mystery person in place of their question. Once the mystery person has been guessed correctly, another player will choose, and the game continues.

TIPS

- If you're guessing, don't guess the mystery person too soon, unless you're absolutely sure. If you do, you'll start to run out of mystery people to choose from far too quickly and the game will have to end!

- Once you've finished a round, go back over the leader's answers and think about why each one fits or doesn't fit. It sparks great conversations about how you think of your friends and family, and really encourages chat that celebrates the people you love. It's also pretty fascinating to see how your idea of a person differs from others' ideas.

NOW TRY THIS

- If you want a slightly more chilled-out version of this game, decide as a group on a person that you all know and go through the categories above, trying to agree on an answer for each one. After a bit of discussion, the players might all agree that Uncle Bob is a cherry tree, for example.

69. No, Mr. Bond, I Expect You to Die

PLAYERS	DIFFICULTY	TIME
2	Hard	20 mins

IN SHORT: Play the criminal mastermind by putting James Bond into an inescapable death trap, or play the spy himself and help him escape! A loose-ruled imagination game.

TAGS: CREATIVE, STORYTELLING, PASS THE TIME, CONVERSATION

WHAT YOU'LL NEED

- Nothing at all (but you might want pen and paper to draw).

HOW TO PLAY

This is not a game you can win or lose. It's more about setting up situations and seeing how the other player can tear them down. It's a great conversation starter and, while I've said it involves two players, you could easily expand this to involve everybody's ideas and theories.

One player is the criminal mastermind, and the other is James Bond. The mastermind **describes the trap** he's put James Bond in, giving as much detail as possible. James Bond may ask as many questions as he needs to get a good picture of where he is.

It is James Bond's job to describe in detail how he'd **escape**. He can use only what is around him, but it is safe to assume that James Bond is very good at picking locks, untying ropes, disarming guards, etc.

The game ends when James Bond is safe and clear of the trap. Then you swap roles and the game begins again.

Here are some elements of a James Bond–style trap that the mastermind could use. However, she'll need to think of the details by herself.

- A tank of piranhas
- A robot with knives for hands
- A slowly moving laser beam
- A car locked on accelerate

- A crashing plane
- A ticking bomb
- A sinking ship
- A furnace

- A pack of wolves
- An angry sumo wrestler
- A wrecking ball
- A burning building

EXAMPLE

Criminal Mastermind: *"You're locked in a steel cage that is slowly lowering into a pool of hungry sharks. Around the side of the pool are six guards armed with pistols. The cage is locked with a padlock and the key thrown away. How do you escape?"*

James Bond: *"Hmm. What am I wearing?"*

Criminal Mastermind: *"You're wearing a set of prison overalls and no shoes."*

James Bond: *"Okay. Because I'm in a cage, the sharks won't actually get me unless I escape, so I'm safe for as long as I can hold my breath. So while I'm underwater I take my nice juicy hand and stick it through the bars right where the padlock is. The sharks will charge at it, but my lightning reflexes mean I can pull it away at the right time and one of them will end up biting the padlock. Okay, so now that I'm free I'll have to punch the sharks on the nose to stun them. The guards will shoot, but I'll swim underwater to the farthest point of the pool and then tug on one guard's leg to pull him in . . ."*

Etc.

TIP

- If you're both intent on winning, this game won't be fun. You'll end up saying a lot of "No, but you can't do that because . . ." In order to make this game work, once the criminal mastermind has given all the information she can, let James Bond take over and enjoy his method. Even if you don't think it would work or know he's forgotten something you've said, don't bring that up until after he's finished his plan. Then you can discuss it and work out a solution together.

70. RPGs (Role-Playing Games)

PLAYERS	DIFFICULTY	TIME
2-5	**Hard**	**2 hours +**

IN SHORT: Days, weeks, months of fun to be had here. An inclusive and imaginative game with literally no boundaries.

TAGS: STORYTELLING, CONVERSATION, COLLABORATIVE, CREATIVE

WHAT YOU'LL NEED

- A notebook and pen (optional, but advised).

WHAT'S A ROLE-PLAYING GAME?

I went to boarding school between the ages of seven and twelve. I was surrounded by boys entirely unlike me, mainly because the only thing allowing me to grace those corridors was a hefty scholarship. Most had land, staff back at home, fathers in the House of Lords, that sort of thing. Fortunately, the vast majority of conversations between boys of that age take place in imaginary worlds: places where I fit in just fine. In those worlds, I was not the odd one out.

Every evening, after lights-out, my dorm-mates and I would play this interactive storytelling game. One boy would play the gamemaster, and everyone else would have roles within the story. Whenever prompted, the characters would have to choose, plan, persuade, argue, voyage, and fight in order to overcome the challenges the storyteller gave them.

Games could last a week of evenings or longer, depending on how engaging they were. Sometimes they reached some sort of happy end, but sometimes the characters would die in horrible, grizzly ways. Most often, we'd all fall asleep and someone else would start a new story the next day.

This game is best for long journeys when you're stuck together and just need somewhere else to be. Given time and attention, it can be absolutely wonderful. My advice is that, considering the time frame it really requires, you shouldn't try this when you have only five minutes to spare or when people are coming and going. You'll never get into it.

HOW TO PLAY

One player is **the gamemaster**. Whoever this is, you'll need to be really confident making up stories and have a good bucket of ideas to dip into. If you haven't already, why not practice your storytelling skills with games like **Genre Bender** or **Switch!** (see pages 60 and 80)? Also, it might help to have read some fantasy novels, such as *The Hobbit*, the *His Dark Materials* trilogy, or *The Wind Singer* for a few ideas. Alternatively, if you've played some of the best console RPGs (anything from the *Legend of Zelda* or *Final Fantasy* series), you'll already have the idea.

The gamemaster begins to tell a story in which the other players are the main characters. So, she'll be using "you" and "your" to talk about the characters' surroundings. It will be as if the other players are living within her story. But here's the great part: throughout the story, it's up to the other players to decide how to act.

The gamemaster should put the other players in difficult situations and let them decide how to get out of it. Together, they'll ask extra questions, decide how to act, and then the gamemaster will react to that with the next part of the story.

Let me give you a quick example.

EXAMPLE

The gamemaster has already explained that the other players are a group of schoolchildren who have been lost in the woods on a school trip, and now the sun is setting.

Gamemaster: *"Okay, so you finished your packed lunches ages ago, and you're starting to feel hungry. At some point you'll need to eat. What are you going to do?"*

Player 1: *"We need to find a way out. Can we see any roads?"*

Gamemaster: *"No, there's just trees and brambles. The brambles are covered in red berries and thorns."*

Player 2: *"I eat some berries!"*

Gamemaster: *"Player 2 eats some berries and feels immediately better. Anybody else want to eat some berries?"*

Player 3: *"No way."*

Gamemaster: *"Hmm. Well, now that I mention it, Player 2 looks a bit pale. You're holding your stomach and rocking your body."*

Player 1: *"She's poisoned! I give her some of my water."*

Player 2: *"I spit out the berries."*

Gamemaster: *"Player 2, you've already swallowed the berries so you can't spit them out, but you do drink the water and you feel a little better. But just as you're catching your breath, you hear howling from the distance."*

Player 1: *"RUN!"*

Etc.

As the gamemaster, it's best to set the scene well. Use your five senses all the time to describe what's around the players. Create dangerous situations for the players to solve, and side characters who send the players on errands and missions: fetching powerful weapons, making useful friends, unlocking doors, making it through dank dungeons, all to get to the final "boss battle" and the conclusion of the story.

The other players should ask lots of questions, to which the gamemaster must give all the information possible. Once they have been filled in, the other players can make group or individual decisions throughout the story. Remember what you've picked up, and use all of your skills to solve problems.

The gamemaster might like to keep track of held items, skills, abilities, and story elements by taking notes on some paper. How about describing the scene by drawing a simple map for the players?

At any point, the gamemaster can tell the players what is or isn't possible. For example, if Player 3 suddenly claims to pull out a bazooka, the gamemaster has every right to remind Player 3 that he doesn't have that weapon.

STORY BASES THAT YOU COULD USE

You're probably still feeling a bit confused by this whole idea. On the following pages, you'll find a few sample stories I've created for you to use. Read through, pick a subject that suits the group you're in, and begin. If you're confident, you'll want to create your own stories. Don't be scared to take inspiration from the worlds you've read about or watched. You can create

Role-Playing Games within the sprawling worlds of Harry Potter or the Marvel comics universe.

Zombie at the Gates

This one is great because you can begin the story in your very own house, and every player can already imagine that setting. The characters wake up and look out the window to see a mob of flesh-eating zombies shambling about. They must gather as many resources as they can carry and venture into the city, fighting off the undead hordes and trying to find safety. Perhaps they could communicate with other survivors over a radio, learn how to protect themselves, break into prisons or police stations to gather armor and weaponry, fix and use a vehicle of their choice, scavenge for food and fuel, and try to set up their own safe zone.

Quest for the Seven Swords

In the fantasy land of Mysteria (a world of dragons, dwarf mines, and corrupt kings), a dark power has taken over. The demonic "Underlord" has risen from the blackness of the underworld to destroy humankind. The players are young elves, each with unique powers. They will have to travel the land, gathering the seven elemental swords that, when united, might be powerful enough to defeat this monstrous beast. The storyteller can create seven different challenges (a jungle land, underwater temple, desert city, fiery tunnels, guarded palace, snowy mountain, sewer system), each hiding its own special sword. Once the players have united them all into a powerful superweapon, they can try to take down the Underlord.

BattleBots

The players are a group of engineers building a fighting robot for the annual "BattleBots" tournament. You let them start with some basic resources and give them some easy opponents to begin with, but as they fight the early rounds they win prize money that can buy them better armor, weaponry, and other items. Each round is a different challenge—the opponents get steadily harder and the arenas are full of dangers. Furthermore, it appears that somebody in the tournament is sabotaging other robots. Can the players win the tournament and the grand prize?

Hunted

The players begin in a bank vault. Tell them that their plan has worked so far—if they can get the money out of the safes and escape, they'll be millionaires. Unfortunately, police surround the vault and the whole city is on lockdown. If they manage to escape the building, they may need to steal a car, escape to the country, and get across the border. Will they survive, or will they be brought to justice?

The Secret of Mettekahu

The players have been dropped from their helicopter deep in the Amazon rain forest with only their backpacks containing basic supplies, and a map to the lost Aztec temple of Mettekahu. If they can survive thieving monkeys and venomous snakes, cross the enormous Amazon River, and fight off a cannibal tribe, then they will reach the temple. Deep inside lies a priceless ruby that would make the players' fortune; however, it is guarded by living stone idols, strange puzzles, and a deadly smoke monster. Can they make it out alive?

CHAPTER 8

AFTER DINNER

For years, you've been idly saying to all your old friends, "Oh, we should do dinner some time," never expecting anything to ever happen. But this time, to their credit, they actually suggested a date. Now the evening has arrived, as have they, with nicer wine than you provided and a bunch of flowers, which is great, but you have no vase. You made chili con carne, because everyone likes chili con carne, except it turns out that Marco isn't into spicy food so he just has the garlic bread.

You've made a playlist, and that goes down well, and your chat about music and films and old pals was great until about dessert, when it morphed, and you got too far into an opinion about politics and now you're finding it hard to back out. Time for a change of pace; something to give the evening its "legendary" status. Time for a game.

Clear the table, pour another glass of wine, and dig into one of these juicy after-dinner treats. They're raucous, challenging, and fresh enough to suggest a round without feeling embarrassed about it. They involve guessing, bluffing, remembering, or creating, but are the kind of activities that'll make an evening last until long after it's acceptable for everyone to just go home.

This chapter also includes my favorite after-dinner game of all time, **1,000 Blank White Cards**, a game so good that my friends organize get-togethers just to play it.

71. 1,000 Blank White Cards

PLAYERS	DIFFICULTY	TIME
3+	Medium	1 hour at least

IN SHORT: A card game that you create as you play.

WHAT YOU'LL NEED

TAGS: CREATIVE, ARTSY, STRATEGY, COMPETITIVE

- Some good-quality card stock, cut into rectangles a little larger than playing cards (something like two-by-three inches). Index cards from a stationery shop work well, cut into two. You'll need around a hundred of these cards for an evening of play, so you must be prepared!

- Pens/pencils for everyone.

- A sheet of paper to keep score.

- Almost anything else, if one of the cards demands it.

HOW TO PLAY

I can't express to you how wonderful this game is. My closest set of friends and I play this as often as we can. It's the perfect mix of silliness, competitiveness, nostalgia, and creativity. Two games can, by definition, never be the same and, best of all, you'll sometimes find yourself in the middle of a game that you never expected to play. Trust me, this is amazing.

Basically, it's a card game that makes itself up as it goes along. The aim, usually, is to score the most points, but we've once had a game that was won by somebody who built a giant robot, and another that resulted in a presidential election.

You'll have a range of cards, some blank, and will take turns playing a card on yourself, your opponent, or the whole table. With the blank cards in your hand, you'll be able to react to the game as a whole and create the cards you need, or just create a card that you think will make your friends laugh.

I'll talk you through the game in phases, but bear in mind, any of this can change at any time if a card commands it.

The Setup: Building Your Deck

If you're playing for the first time, then this will take a little longer, but it's a lot of fun in itself, so don't worry.

Every game starts with **52 cards** in a stack at the center of the table. This should be made of:

- **26 old cards** voted through from the previous game;

- **14 blank white cards**;

- **12 new cards** that you'll create right now, in the setup.

If it's your first game, then the pile should look like this:

- **32 new cards** that you'll create right now, in the setup;

- **20 blank white cards**.

Notice that the game will begin with **blank cards** in the deck for you to fill as you go, but you'll also create some now, before the game begins.

To do this, divide out the right number of blank cards (**32** if it's your first game, **12** if it isn't) so that each player has an even number, or close to it. Then, allow five to ten minutes for each player to fill their cards and place them facedown on top of the deck in the middle of the table.

What Should I Put on My Cards?

A basic card should have a title, a picture, and some sort of text. It should have writing/drawing on one side only. That said, there really is no rule. Here are a few types of card that you could think about:

- *Challenges:* Give a player a task in order to earn some points, or to avoid losing any. It could be some sort of dare, acting performance, physical challenge, or memory task. The card on the right is the oldest surviving card in our deck. I don't even want to imagine how many people have licked it.

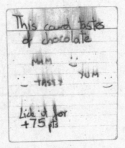

- *New Rules:* Change the way that the game is played, subtly or significantly. You could change the order of play, have someone lose their turn, or even change how a player actually wins the game. In the example on the right, one player becomes the Thumb Master and has a new role to play.

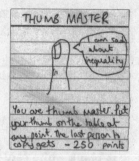

- *Anything Else:* Don't be limited by rules and regulations. Your card could give somebody a secret mission, or just be pretty. It could apply to everyone or one person. It could, if you want, just be a drawing. Do what you want!

It feels wrong to give you too many examples, because this game thrives on originality, but if I can help you get off the ground, then that's excellent. Here are a few more cards in my archive for a little inspiration.

Once you've played, please, please share your best cards with me on Twitter @IvanBrett. I want to make a hall-of-fame deck out of other people's genius creations.

The Game Begins

Make sure you now have the right number of old, new, and blank cards in the deck. Shuffle the deck, then deal 5 cards, facedown, to each player.

One player needs to keep score on a piece of paper, although this is quite a difficult job. Everyone should be involved in making sure the scores keep updating correctly.

The player who was the ugliest baby moves first, by playing a card faceup in front of any of the players, including himself or herself, or to the center of the table. The instructions on the card then apply to the person who received the card. So, the receiver might earn some points, or have to do a certain task. Finally, the player should pick up a new card from the face-down deck in the center of the table, to finish her turn.

It's hard to tell you the rules when any card could change them. But . . . generally, play moves clockwise (unless it doesn't) and players play one card in front of another player, then pick one up (unless they don't). Players can't pick up any card that has already been played (unless they can).

Cards that award points stay in front of you on the table but don't keep on acting, while cards with persistent effects (such as "Talk like a horse") continue to act until the end of the game, or until another card overrides them.

At any point in the game, if you have a blank card in your hand, you may write or draw on it. It's best to save these blank cards so that you can react to other cards already on the table. For example, if somebody has played a card on your side of the table that says "The Floor Is Lava! Keep your body off the floor," you might make a card that says "Sudden Snowfall. The ground hardens up," and play that card on top when it's your turn. Generally, if a card is covered up by another card played on top, the covered-up card no longer does anything. But . . . it's up to you!

If at any point it isn't clear how a card should work, decide as a group. This can happen from time to time, but it often creates the most interesting moments.

You'll find very quickly that it's not worth trying to win, particularly. I could easily write "You win!" on a card and play it on myself, but within seconds somebody else will have made a card that says "No you don't" and played that on top. In truth, if you're trying to win, you're probably playing the wrong game.

The End of the Game

The game ends when there are no more cards to play (or maybe another way if the cards say so). At this point, the player keeping the score should announce the winner, the loser, and any other accolades or awards that have been earned through the game. In one game, there were three different types of points to be won, so while I won the "points" game, Isaac won the most money and John got the most puppies.

Whatever the case, it's time to collect all the cards and move on to the final stage of the game:

Review Phase

This stage is very enjoyable and really important, so don't skip it! One player takes turns showing each card to the table, and you jointly decide if it will be used in the next game. Remember, every game starts with 26 cards held through from the last game.

Think about voting for not necessarily the funniest card, but the ones that will function best in the next game. Some cards were brilliant in the previous game, but might be too powerful or not meaningful enough for the next game. Once you've agreed on 26, keep them ready for the next time you play. It's worth keeping an archive of rejected cards too, as it's hugely entertaining to look back through them later.

This game is as much fun as you make it. Some people will crave more rigid rules, or get frustrated if they make good cards and don't win. But give it time, and this game will reward you more than any other in this book. Plus, once you get started, it's really hard to stop. It'll eat up your evening in an absolute flash.

72. Category Scramble

PLAYERS	DIFFICULTY	TIME
2+	Medium	1 hour

IN SHORT: An alphabet categories game. Think of
words that fit into each category before the time
runs out.

TAGS:
VOCABULARY,
STRATEGY,
COMPETITIVE

WHAT YOU'LL NEED

• Paper and pencil for each player.

• List of categories (see pages 251–52), photocopied or
  written out, then cut up, folded, and mixed in a hat.

• The letters of the alphabet, cut up and placed in another hat (don't
  bother with Q, U, V, X, Y, or Z—too hard!). Alternatively, you could use
  an online alphabet spinner.

• Countdown timer.

• Access to a search engine to check answers.

HOW TO PLAY

In each round you'll need to select some random categories from your hat.
How many you choose is up to you, but five is a nice round number. Place
them in the middle of the table where every player can see them.

Next, one player should randomly pick a letter from the other hat, read
it aloud to the group, and **immediately** begin the timer. I recommend
one minute, but again, it's up to the group to decide.

In the time given, each player should try to write down just one word or
short phrase for each category that begins with this round's letter. If there
are five categories, then each player should write the numbers 1–5 in a column
on their paper, to make it clear which guess is for which category.

After the time is up, players compare their answers. It might be necessary to check if some answers are correct or not, using a search engine. If it's still unclear, make a joint decision as a team. You get a point for each correct answer. In my opinion, a bit of incorrect spelling should not matter in this game, as long as the answer is clear enough.

First person to 50 points wins. Or 20 points. Or 40,000. Who am I to tell you when to finish your game?

EXAMPLE

*The categories chosen were **Superheroes**, **Vegetables**, **Movies**, **Things You Hide**, and **Enormous Things**. The letter was **S**.*

Player 1 wrote down:	Player 2 wrote down:
Superman	1. Spider-Man
Salad	2. Sweet onion
Scream	3. San Andreas
Sugar	4. Smile
Space	5. —

*The players decide that salad isn't a type of vegetable because it can contain all sorts of ingredients, and that there's no real reason to hide sugar. Player 1 argues that there is often hidden sugar in processed food. The others agree to give her the point. She gets **4** overall.*

*For Player 2's answers, the others use the Internet to search "sweet onion" and are surprised to find that it is a type of onion! As for San Andreas, again the Internet confirms that it is a film (a terrible film, but still a film). Player 2 says that he has to hide his smile in class or he gets detention, so he also gets **4** points.*

TIP

- If you get stuck, think of two-word phrases that might fit the category. Kitchen scissors is a household item that begins with "k," even if scissors begins with "s."

NOW TRY THIS

- If you have lots of players, why not introduce a rule whereby you get a point only if *nobody else guesses* the same answer as you? So if two people choose Superman, neither gets the point. It will encourage you to think of more unusual answers. Because of this new challenge, you may need a little more time per round.

- I have seen this game played where any player at any time can shout "STOP THE CLOCK!," at which point the round immediately ends. If the shouting player wins, they get double points for the round, but if they don't win the round, or if it's a tie, they get **no points at all**. Is it worth the risk?

73. Would You Rather?

PLAYERS	DIFFICULTY	TIME
2+	Easy	20 mins +

IN SHORT: Would you rather have toes instead of fingers, or fingers instead of hair?

TAGS:
CREATIVE,
CONVERSATION,
WIND-DOWN

WHAT YOU'LL NEED

- Nothing at all.

HOW TO PLAY

There is no stranger way to digest your food than over a round or two of this choices game. Having said that, it's huge amounts of fun, and encourages you to be very creative.

One player chooses **two** possibilities that are either both really horrible or really great. She then offers them to the other players in the form "Would you rather _____ or _____?"

The rest of the players should discuss and decide which option they would prefer. It works best if you really follow through with the idea. What would it be like on the first day/a week after/twenty years after?

. . . And the game continues. The only competition is coming up with the best "Would You Rather?" questions.

EXAMPLE

Start with these, then create your own:

- *Would you rather freeze every time it's cold, or melt every time it's hot?*
- *Would you rather know everything about the future, or everything about the past?*
- *Would you rather sing every time you want to speak, or laugh every time you want to cry?*

- *Would you rather have one elephant-sized leg or two duck-sized legs?*

- *Would you rather have the power to talk to animals, or the power to connect your brain to the Internet?*

- *Would you rather be hated and rich, or loved and penniless?*

- *Would you rather never eat chocolate again in your life, or have everything in the world turn into chocolate?*

- *Would you rather spend the rest of your life inside or outside?*

- *Would you rather eat the same food at every meal for the rest of your life (your choice) or never eat the same dish twice (you never choose)?*

- *Would you rather own a dragon or be a dragon?*

- *Would you rather be able to fly or be able to breathe underwater?*

- *Would you rather have feet instead of hands, or fingers instead of hair?*

- *Would you rather read people's minds or be able to put thoughts inside people's minds?*

- *Would you rather have an elephant's trunk or a giraffe's neck?*

- *Would you rather be stuck in a room with the dirty socks of everyone who ran the London Marathon, or run the London Marathon in bare feet?*

74. Wavy Gravy

PLAYERS	DIFFICULTY	TIME
2+	Medium	30 mins

IN SHORT: Find pairs of rhyming words that should never go together . . . and watch as the other players explain how they do.

TAGS: RHYME, CONVERSATION, COLLABORATIVE, CREATIVE

WHAT YOU'LL NEED

• Nothing at all.

HOW TO PLAY

Thanks to my old pal Charlie for this one. It's perfect for those long, rambling after-dinner conversations.

Players come up with a pair of rhyming words, such as "Wavy Gravy." The only rule is that the words shouldn't go well together, in terms of meaning. So "Fat Cat" or "Cool Pool" aren't good here. It's pretty obvious how you can have an overweight cat or, for that matter, a nice cool swimming pool. I actually have one of those two things. (Spoiler: it's the cat.)

So, a pair of rhyming but unlikely words. "Rock Clock" would be a good one, or "Flyin' Lion."

Now, it's every other player's chance to prove how wrong you are. The words do fit together! "Wavy Gravy" is a commonly seen thing! They might explain how, in the government's underground gravy reservoir, where the meaty sauce is saved up in case of a nuclear war, they have to keep the liquid agitated so that it doesn't go moldy. So they've installed a wave machine, making the surface of the gravy constantly wavy.

Or, for "Rock Clock," perhaps one player would mention that the stone statue of Nelson in Trafalgar Square actually has a working watch on his wrist. It's made entirely of granite and is powered by a "hard rock current" (AC/DC, apparently).

And "Flyin' Lion"'s not really a rare pair of words. The reason lions sleep all day is because at night they creep up behind vultures and latch their claws into their feathers. When the vultures fly away, the lions get a lift, up into the clouds, for a refreshing nighttime journey. It's actually a fairly common sight in the African savannah.

As you can see, this game has a pretty free structure. The basic model of play is that whatever rare rhyming pair a player thinks of, the other players assure her that, in fact, it's common as muck. If this branches off into discussions of how much underground gravy is *too much* underground gravy, then that's mission accomplished.

The winner of the game is the first person to have a really enjoyable evening.

TIP

- This game is all collaboration, no competition. Once a player's had a really good go at describing why the phrase is a common one (and only when they're finished), add your own seasoning to the pot with any more detail or explanation that struck you as they were speaking. Just make sure you only ever *accept* and *build*. Don't contradict anything that the other player has said, or you'll end up competing to have the best idea.

75. Two Truths and a Lie

PLAYERS	DIFFICULTY	TIME
2+	Medium	30 mins

IN SHORT: Give three statements. One is a lie. Can the other players guess which?

TAGS:
CREATIVE,
GUESSING,
STRATEGY,
CONVERSATION

WHAT YOU'LL NEED

* Paper and pencils to record the scores and write down your statements, if you aren't good at remembering them.

HOW TO PLAY

This game is really good if you don't know your dinner guests very well but you want to change that. If you think you do in fact know everything about your dinner guests, this game might help to teach you that you don't!

To begin, one player, the first "liar," should think about **two true facts** about themselves that the other players won't know. If you're the liar, you could think about the things you've done in your life, the places you've been, or the people you've met. You should then make up **a false fact**: something that sounds like it could be true, when in reality it's total nonsense. Practice saying each one in your head, making the lie sound like the true ones.

Now the liar should say all three of their statements, with the lie popped in at random.

It's everyone else's job to call out the lie. Each player gets to make a guess, and after they've all done so, the liar reveals which was false. Every player who guessed it correctly gets a point, and the liar gets a point for every person he managed to fool.

Note down the scores on a piece of paper, and then another person becomes the liar for the next round. Try at least four sets of statements per player before tallying the final scores.

EXAMPLE

Liar: *"All right, here are my three statements:*
   A: I used to have an imaginary friend called Dirtyfeet, who was a bull.
   B: I have ridden on a tame bull called Pavel.
   C: I was once chased around a beach by a bull."
Guesser 1: *"I think it's C. Why was a bull on a beach?"*
Guesser 2: *"I'm going for B. I'd know if you did that."*
Guesser 3: *"Yeah, good point. I'm going B."*
Liar: *"Yep, the lie was B."*

So, Guessers 2 and 3 get a point each for guessing correctly, while the Liar gets 1 point for fooling Guesser 1.

TIPS

- Notice how after Guesser 2 said that she knew the answer, she made it easier for Guesser 3. Don't give anything away until after the answers have been revealed! You don't want others getting points because of your knowledge. It might even help if you pretend to be unsure . . .

- If you can't think of a lie, try making all your facts related in some way. Notice how all of the ones above were about bulls.

- It may be obvious, but make sure that your truths and lie aren't always in the same order! There's a bit of game theory to this, so I have to be careful what I say. Basically, wherever you'd normally put your lie . . . don't put it there. Or, if people think you won't, then do. Or something. I'm confused.

NOW TRY THIS

- If you're ready to move on, how about this one: every player thinks of a significant item from their past. It could be a teddy bear, your rattly old scooter, or the tree in your childhood garden. However, if you want, you could make up a completely false item. Whether it's true or false, describe the item to the other players, explaining why it's important to you, what you used to do with it, where it is now, and so on. After you've finished, the other players should decide if this is a real item or not. It works well because for those who choose to lie, it's wonderful fun to pretend to be all nostalgic about something you've just created.

- I heard an episode of the Adam Buxton podcast where he and the comedian Jayde Adams played a brilliant variation of this game using children you remember from your school days. Pick the names of two real kids you remember from a year at school and make up another. You could just say their full names, or add a little sentence about them. The other players have to guess which is the made-up child. Making up fake names is such fun, especially if you have to build a little character around them, too. (If you *really* like this version of the game, be an author. Making up little side characters is part of our daily routine.)

76. No More Dogs

PLAYERS	DIFFICULTY	TIME
2+	Hard	Ongoing

IN SHORT: Pick from a shrinking selection of famous names, then make it even harder for your opponent.

TAGS:
MEMORY,
STRATEGY,
CIRCLE GAMES

WHAT YOU'LL NEED

- Nothing at all.

HOW TO PLAY

This is a naming game with a twist, which owes its existence to the British comedians Mark Watson, Alex Horne, and Tim Key. It's simple to learn but difficult to play. Groups of adults will get more from this than children, as a guide.

The first player names a well-known character (alive, dead, real, fictional, anything), and then **eliminates** everybody else in that category. For example, she might say, "Queen Elizabeth II. No more women."

The next player must name somebody who hasn't been eliminated yet, and then impose a new rule, and so on and so forth until one player cannot name a person who follows within all of the rules.

EXAMPLE

Player 1: "Queen Elizabeth II. No more women."
   (Player 2 has just one rule to follow, so it's pretty easy right now.)
Player 2: "Scooby Doo. No more dogs."
   (Player 3's job is still pretty easy: no women or dogs.)
Player 3: "Gary Barlow. No more English people."
Player 4: "Andy Murray. No more real people."
Player 1: "Count Dracula. No more names beginning with C."

   (By this point, Player 2 has a lot to remember. He needs to think of a non-female, non-dog, non-English, non-real, non-C-beginning character.)

Player 2: *"Harry Potter?"*

But Harry Potter is English! Player 2 loses this round.

TIPS

- There are two different types of rules. Some rules eliminate most possible answers. These make the game difficult, but they aren't hard to remember. Then, there are the sleeper rules that everybody forgets about, because they don't eliminate many answers. Then, five minutes later, somebody names a dog and loses.

- If someone's already eliminated dead people, don't eliminate living people. All you would have left are zombies, and nobody wants that. The same goes for real/fictional, young/old, and all the other binary descriptions. Be more creative!

- Don't forget, the rule can be anything from descriptions of the person to the spelling of their name. Don't limit it to their job.

NOW TRY THIS

- This game was originally played by Watson, Horne, and Key with a chess timer. Every time you say a word, you hit your button, start the opponent's timer, and put the pressure on them. If they run out of time, they lose. It's a more stressful version of the game and it requires a chess timer (which I certainly don't have!), but it looks like fun.

77. Acrophobia

PLAYERS	DIFFICULTY	TIME
1+	Hard	10 mins per word

IN SHORT: Competitive acronyms game.

WHAT YOU'LL NEED

- Pen and paper.

TAGS:
CREATIVE,
SILLY,
COMPETITIVE

HOW TO PLAY

An acronym is a word formed from the first letters of a phrase. So, for example, **UK** stands for United Kingdom and **SCUBA** stands for Self-Contained Underwater Breathing Apparatus. Who knew?

In this game, you'll be making acronyms in reverse. Simply, one player, the judge, will come up with a random string of letters (between three and six works best) and write it on a napkin or a piece of paper, placing it in the center of the table where all other players can see it. All the other players must come up with a phrase or sentence in which the first letters of each word make the acronym.

You could write down your acronym, but why not just work it out in your head? It'll be easier to change and edit your ideas, plus you'll use fewer napkins and save the planet.

After one minute, each player must tell their acronym sentence to the group. Players can comment on which they like, but it's the judge who picks a winner. She could choose the funniest, the one that sounds most like a real acronym, or the most creative.

If you want to keep score, the winner of the round gets 1 point. I advise not bothering with a score, but just handing the napkin to the winner of the round, so that they can make up the letters for the next acronym, and so on.

EXAMPLE

The judge writes down the letters "PCNLR." Each player thinks for around one minute, or until they all look ready.

Player 1: *"Please Can Nigel Learn Russian?"*
Player 2: *"Powdered Cheese: Now Less Rubbery!"*
Player 3: *"Poets for the Creation of Nasty and Lame Rhymes."*

The judge decides that she prefers Player 2's sentence, so now he takes the napkin for the next round.

TIPS

- Your acronym could be a simple, funny sentence like Player 1's, or it could act like the title of a group, movement, or project, like Player 3's.

- If you're getting stuck, first go to the "rarest" letter and decide what that will be.

- Also remember that you can have little unimportant words between your main words that go into the acronym, just like Player 3 did. It's less satisfying, and people might not like it as much, but it's done all the time in real life.

NOW TRY THIS

- If there are lots of you (at least six), and you each have pieces of paper, it's possible to play a slightly more complicated version of this game. Here everyone writes down their sentence secretly, then hands their paper to the judge. The judge now reads out the sentences in a random order, and the rest of the players vote on which is their favorite. Obviously, you can't vote for your own sentence. The player with the most votes gets a point and makes up the letters for the next round.

78. Fictionary

PLAYERS	DIFFICULTY	TIME
2+	Hard	30 mins +

IN SHORT: An after-dinner definitions game. Tremendous fun!

TAGS: WRITING, GRAMMAR, WIND-DOWN

WHAT YOU'LL NEED

- As many dictionaries as possible. (You can also use www.randomword.com for your random word needs!)

- Pencils and paper for every player.

- A way to hide your paper. Lean on a big book or use clipboards.

HOW TO PLAY

This game takes a little time, but it's great for those cozy post-meal scenarios where everyone just needs to loosen up a little.

Pass the dictionary around the room. Each player should flick to a random page and find a word that they think the others will not know. Without anybody else seeing, write that **word**, as well as **its definition**, on your paper.

Now, create two more fake definitions for this word. Try to make them as formal and grown-up as the definition from the dictionary. The aim is to convince the other players that one of your made-up definitions is the real one.

Pay attention to the word type. Whether your word is a noun (a thing), a verb (an action), or an adjective (a description), make sure your fake definitions are that, too.

Once everybody is ready with their words, the first player reads his word a couple of times, then the three definitions. Make sure to vary the order of your definitions, so that you don't always read the real one first.

The other players must choose which is the real definition. This is a team game, so you must come to a decision as a group. Then the player reveals the real definition. If she managed to fool the group, she gets a point; otherwise nobody does. Go around the circle until everybody has had a turn. Then begin again.

EXAMPLE

Quinzhee. It's a noun. But what does it mean?
>   *A: A five-wheeled carriage.*
>   *B: A type of crossbow.*
>   *C: A snow shelter.*
>*(Answer: C! If you got it wrong, then I get a point.)*

TIP

- Make sure to practice reading the real definition. If you get stuck on a word when reading it aloud, it's really obvious that you didn't write it and everybody will call your bluff.

79. Botticelli

PLAYERS	DIFFICULTY	TIME
2+	Hard	20-30 mins

IN SHORT: A fun "guess the celeb"-style game, with some interesting rules.

TAGS:
MEMORY,
CIRCLE GAMES,
WIND-DOWN

WHAT YOU'LL NEED

- Nothing at all.

HOW TO PLAY

I've marked this as a "hard" game, because your knowledge of famous people and their names needs to be pretty good. Kids could have a go, but they might find it a little frustrating.

One player, the celebrity, decides to be any famous person from history or the present day. For this game to work, it should be somebody whom all the other players know about and could name.

The celebrity gives one clue to begin: the initial letter of the mystery person's surname. "My surname begins with S," she might say.

Now it is time for the other players to guess who the celebrity is. However, their style of question is limited: they must ask a yes-or-no question that would lead to that person's name. So, for example, if the guesser wanted to guess Arnold Schwarzenegger, he might ask, "Did you play the Terminator?"

Now, three things could happen:

- If the guesser is right, then the celebrity responds, "Yes, I am Arnold Schwarzenegger!" and the guesser wins. He is the celebrity for the next turn.

- If the guesser is wrong but the celebrity knows whom he's talking about, then she must respond, "No, I am not Arnold Schwarzenegger," and then the next guesser gets to guess.

- However, if the celebrity doesn't know whom the guesser is asking about, then the guesser gets to ask a free question about the secret person. (Any question is allowed, so long as the answer wouldn't have to include all or part of the celebrity's name.) So the guesser might now ask "How old are you?" or "What are you famous for?" The celebrity's response will help narrow down the other players' next guesses.

This is a fun game to play because it puts requirements on every player. The guessers must think of celebrities with that initial letter, while the celebrities must follow clues to work out who the guessers are guessing. There are a few moving parts, though, so if you're confused, look at this example.

EXAMPLE

(Player 1 has picked Winston Churchill.)

Player 1: *"My surname begins with C."*

Player 2: *"All right. Were you in black-and-white movies?"*

Player 1: *"No, I'm not Charlie Chaplin."*

Player 3: *"Okay, did you sing 'All I Want for Christmas Is You'?"*

Player 1: *"No, I'm not . . . erm . . ."*

Player 3: *"Mariah Carey! That means I get a free question. What nationality are you?"*

Player 1: *"British."*

Player 4: *"Okay, so do you judge The X Factor?"*

Player 1: *"No, I'm not Simon Cowell."*

Player 2: *"Do you play James Bond?"*

Player 1: *"Ooh, I know his name . . . I do . . . darn. Dunno."*

Player 2: *"Daniel Craig! Right, free question. What is your job?"*

Player 1: *"I'm a politician."*

Player 3: *"Ooh, I know! Did you help Britain win World War II?"*

Player 1: *"Yes! I'm Winston Churchill!"*

TIPS

- Go through different jobs that famous people might have with the letter "C" held firmly in your head.

- Go through the alphabet of your *second choice*. "Ca, Cb, Cc, Cd," etc. It might help you think of surnames.

80. Hunt for the Pair

PLAYERS	DIFFICULTY	TIME
5+	Hard	15 mins per round

IN SHORT: Two players are given a secret word and must identify each other. The other players must bluff to look like they have the word.

TAGS: GUESSING, STRATEGY, COMPETITIVE

WHAT YOU'LL NEED

- Lots of slips of paper, small, but not too small. Standard copier paper cut into quarters is perfect. If you have tiny handwriting, you could cut each piece into eighths.

- An additional piece of paper to keep score.

- Pencil or pen for each player.

HOW TO PLAY

This game is excellent, but a little complicated. Bear with me on this one, and use the example for clarification. It has excellent replay value, but the first couple of times you play you'll need somebody to know these rules really well.

One player will be the dealer for this turn. Each turn, this role passes to the left, so everybody will have to be the dealer eventually.

The Setup

The dealer takes a slip of paper for every other player (if there are four other players, she takes four slips of paper). Without any other players seeing, she chooses **one random word** and writes it at the top of *two* of the slips of paper. On the others, she writes the word "BLUFF." The dealer needs to leave space on the paper for something else later, so she must not take up all the space. Finally, the dealer shuffles the slips of paper so that the secret words and the bluffs are in a random order.

Now, all the other players put out their hands and **close their eyes**, and the dealer hands out the slips of paper facedown (or folded). As soon as each player has their slip, they can look at their word, taking care not to let anyone else see. Two players, the pair, will have the secret word, and the rest will have "BLUFF."

Here's where the fun begins. If you are one of the pair, your aim is to discover your partner and identify yourself to them, without giving it away to the bluffers. If you are a bluffer, your aim is to work out who has the words at the same time as convincing others that *you* have the secret word. There are two identical rounds, which work as follows:

Round 1

Starting with the player to the left of the dealer, each player must say just one word that links to the secret word. So, if you are one of the pair, and it is "ball," you might say "goal" or "inflate." Hopefully, your counterpart will pick up on your link.

If you are a bluffer, then you won't know what word to link to. You'll have to say any word that sounds like it might link. Use other people's words as a guide here. Of course, if you have to say your word first, and you're bluffing, you're at a disadvantage because you have absolutely nothing to go on. On the plus side, you might be able to spot a few bluffers if they say words that link to your made-up one.

Once every player has said one word, Round 1 ends. Every player may choose at this point to guess on their slip who the two players with the secret word are. (If you have the secret word, you already know one of them!) Bear in mind, though, that if you vote in Round 1, you may not vote in Round 2.

If you wish to vote, write "Round 1:" and then the two names of the pair. If you do not, write "Round 1: No Vote." Whatever the case, keep your slip of paper secret until the end of the whole game. You may not make half your vote in Round 1 and half in Round 2. And you earn points only if you get both names right. It's all or nothing.

Round 2

In the same order, say just one word. By this point, if you are a bluffer, you may have more of an idea what the secret word is.

After the second round, everybody gets their final chance to vote. If you have not already voted, write "Round 2:" and then the two names of the pair. If you already voted in Round 1, write "Round 2: No Vote."

Finally, all bluffers get one chance to guess the mystery word. They must write it as such at the bottom of their paper like so: "The word is: . . ."

The Reveal

Now the game is over. One by one, players should turn over their slips of paper, revealing if they were bluffing or if they had the secret word, and what their guess was. The scoring works as follows:

- **Correct guess of the pair in Round 1:** 3 points

- **Correct guess of the pair in Round 2:** 2 points

- **Correct guess of the secret word (bluffers only):** 1 point

Important: The pair who have the secret word get their points only if BOTH PLAYERS guess correctly.

After the points have been added to the scores by the dealer, the role passes to the left, and another round begins.

EXAMPLE

The dealer writes "APPLE" on two of the pieces of paper and "BLUFF" on the rest. Once they have all received their paper and secretly read the word, the game begins. Player 2 and Player 5 find that they are the pair. Notice how the bluffers use any clue to try to appear like the pair, while the pair try to blend in.

Player 1: *"Black."*
Player 2: *"Blackberry."*
Player 3: *"Mud."*
Player 4: *"Plum."*
Player 5: *"Snake."*

At the end of Round 1, Player 3 takes the risk for a bigger score and writes "Round 1: Player 2 and Player 4." He will get 0 points for this. Everyone else writes "Round 1: No Vote." Nobody knows anybody else's votes yet, though.

In the second round, everybody has a better idea of the secret word, so the guesses get closer.

Player 1: *"Orange."*
Player 2: *"Core."*
Player 3: *"Tree."*
Player 4: *"Apple."*
Player 5: *"Pip."*

Players 2 and **5** *know it isn't* **Player 4***, because she said the actual word.* **Player 5** *writes down, "Round 2:* **Players 2** and **5***," but even though he's correct,* **Player 2** *has written, "Round 2:* **Players 2** and **3***," so neither gets any points.* **Player 1** *guesses "Round 2:* **Players 2** and **5***. The word is: apple." He gets 3 points: 2 for a correct guess in Round 2, and 1 for the correct word.*

TIP

- The best thing about this game is that you can develop all sorts of tactics. Would it benefit you to pretend you had the secret word if you actually don't? Would it benefit you to pretend you're bluffing when in fact you know the word? The game changes with the people playing it, which is great.

CHAPTER 9

A VERY MERRY CHRISTMAS*

Christmas: a day that's been looming since October, and it's finally here. This morning, after presents, you climbed into your best apron and got on with the annual turkey-wrestle, using that fun new recipe where you stick a can of beer up its butt. Your parents arrived too early, so Mom spent the whole morning commenting on your culinary skills and Dad popped open the drinks cabinet rather too soon. Your brother and his wife and their baby arrived next, whom you all love but can't hug because your hands are covered in turkey juice.

Anyway, Christmas lunch for nine came together well. The potatoes were particularly crispy. Yes, Dad choked on a pig-in-a-blanket and knocked over a quite large glass of red wine in the commotion, but you're all full and the Christmas pudding's been roundly ignored, which can only be a good sign.

Somehow, you all roll yourselves into the living room, and then there's that awful moment of realization that nobody has anything to do for the rest of the day. The queen's speech is about to start on TV, and the fear is that once she's been switched on, nobody will have the energy to turn her off again.

But it's okay. I have just the answer. In this chapter are ten games that you can play on a lazy festive afternoon with all the in-laws and cousins, with no movement required. So curl up by a Netflix stream of a crackling fire, climb into your warmest sweater, and crack open one of the games in this chapter.

They're fun for everyone, even more so accompanied by a sherry. Each has massive repeat value, but nobody's going to be asked to dance around or do an animal impression. These are full-belly, curtains-drawn, sofa-full-of-family games that everyone will enjoy.

* The "merry" part of this chapter is essential. The "Christmas" not so. These games are great for any family occasion, especially ones where baby, it's cold outside.

81. One-Word Story

PLAYERS	DIFFICULTY	TIME
2+	Easy	5–20 mins

IN SHORT: Quick-fire storytelling game that never fails to be hilarious.

WHAT YOU'LL NEED

TAGS:
STORYTELLING,
VOCABULARY,
CIRCLE GAMES,
SILLY

- Nothing at all.

HOW TO PLAY

This game involves taking turns, so first of all, decide on an order of play. Clockwise around the room would work.

One player begins by saying the first word of a story. Then the next player will say the next, followed by another word by the third player, and so on.

This is really a top tip, but it's so important that it has to go here: **always accept what's come before and build upon it**. Every time you play this game, you'll have your own idea of where the story **should** go. Unfortunately, other players may have different ideas and take a turn you didn't want. Whichever twist or turn the story takes, just go with it and enjoy the ride.

The game ends whenever feels right! If it begins to trail off, wait until the person before you says "the" and then use the word "end." That seems to work.

EXAMPLE

Player 1: "Once"
Player 2: "upon"
Player 3: "a"
Player 4: "time".
Player 1: "there"
Player 2: "was"
Player 3: "a"
Player 4: "werewolf . . ."
Etc.

TIPS

- There are two ways that this game ends up going: crazy or sensible. Both are great, and I won't say that one is better than the other, BUT sometimes in a game you'll get almost everybody trying to make a sensible story and one person simply saying "werewolf" every time it's their turn. Unless everyone's being crazy, don't be the werewolf guy! It's not going to make the game fun for anybody apart from you.

- When everyone's dying to have a say in the story, it's frustrating if you keep getting forced to say the dull words like "of." Don't worry—your time will come . . .

82. Twenty Questions (aka Animal, Vegetable, Mineral)

PLAYERS	DIFFICULTY	TIME
2+	Easy	10 mins per round

IN SHORT: The well-known guessing game that requires players to ask meaningful questions to discover the answer.

TAGS: STRATEGY, GUESSING, CONVERSATION, PASS THE TIME

WHAT YOU'LL NEED

- Nothing at all.

HOW TO PLAY

This game is perfect for Christmas because it's so easy to get involved. Everybody can have guesses, and nobody has to leave their warm spot on the sofa.

One player, the picker, picks an item in the world. It could be **animal** (including anything made from animals), **vegetable** (all plants, including anything made from plants, e.g., a wooden spoon), or **mineral** (the rest, basically—anything that isn't alive and was never alive). They must keep this word a secret.

The guessers may now ask up to twenty questions to discover the secret item. They can all chip in whenever they want; they don't need to take turns. Traditionally, the first question is, "Animal, Vegetable, or Mineral?" to which the picker must answer with at least one of the three words. After that, **every other question must be given only a yes-or-no answer**. The picker may not say anything other than these two words, even if the guesser tries to ask a different sort of question.

Keep track on your fingers of the number of questions you've asked.

The guessers can guess at the item whenever they like, but that counts as one of their twenty questions.

If the twenty questions pass and the guessers have not guessed correctly, the game is over and the picker could reveal the answer, then pick another word. If one of the guessers does guess the word correctly, then they become the picker.

EXAMPLE

Guesser 1: "Animal, vegetable, or mineral?"

Picker: "Animal."

Guesser 2: "Is it alive?"

Picker: "Yes."

Guesser 3: "Can you keep it as a pet?"

Picker: "No."

Guesser 2: "Does it live in the sea?"

Picker: "Yes."

Guesser 1: "How big is it?"

Picker: "NO!" (It wasn't a yes-or-no question.)

Guesser 1: "Okay, you bore. Is it really big?"

Picker: "Yes!"

Guesser 1: "Is it a whale?"

Picker: "Yes! You did it in seven questions!"

TIPS

- Before you begin, make sure everybody agrees what you can and cannot choose:

  1. Can you choose a particular person, rather than just "human," as your answer?

  2. Can you choose something imaginary or a character on TV?

  3. Do animal products like milk and leather count as animal or mineral? (My advice is animal, but you decide!)

- Some items are more than one thing. For example, a shoe has animal (leather from a cow), vegetable (rubber sole from a rubber tree), and mineral (metal strap buckle). If this is the case, the picker should answer the first question with "Animal, vegetable, *and* mineral."

- If you fancy yourself an expert at this game, you'll be trying to get the answer in as few questions as possible. The following is an experimental and risky tactic that can drastically reduce the number of guesses you take, as long as you're ready to employ a bit of Boolean logic. It's based on that proven tactic to always win "Guess Who?" Basically, you ask two questions at once. "Does it swim in the ocean OR fly in the air?" If the answer is no, you've chopped off two possible categories in one question. "Is it made of wood AND worth more than a hundred dollars?" If the answer is yes, you have found out two important facts about the item.

- Of course, this tactic relies on all players understanding the real meanings of AND and OR. For an OR question to have the answer "yes," only one part of the question needs to be true, but if both are true you'll get the answer "yes" as well. For an AND question to have the answer "yes," both parts of the question must be true. For more on this topic, ask a pedant.

NOW TRY THIS

- You could instigate a "winner stays on" rule, where for as long as you get a yes answer, you may ask another question. This is fun but really not necessary, as it makes the game a little more about yourself and less about the group.

83. Say What You See

PLAYERS	DIFFICULTY	TIME
2+	Easy	Up to 1 hour

IN SHORT: Guess what's being drawn the fastest, and
it's your turn to draw!

TAGS:
ARSTY,
STRATEGY,
GUESSING,
GRAMMAR

WHAT YOU'LL NEED

- Paper or mini whiteboard, large enough for
  everyone to see, and pencil/dry-erase marker.

- List of words (Ideas Bank 2, 3, and 4 on pages 231–39)
  printed and cut up.

- Optional: colored pencils, felt tips, or a drawing app on a tablet.

HOW TO PLAY

The best thing about this game is that it can be as simple or as difficult as
you want to make it.

At its simplest, one player, the artist, **draws a word** from the hat (or chooses
one) and attempts to draw it for the other players. The guessers' aim is to
guess the word. The artist may not use any words, letters, or numbers in her
image, and she may not speak at all. The guessers may shout out as many
guesses as they like, but the first to guess the correct word wins the round,
gets a point, and is next to draw.

If you want a challenge, then there's a quick twist that makes this game
way better. I didn't put this in the **Now Try This** section because I think it's
really worth trying once you're confident with the game.

The twist is this: choose to ban common and proper nouns. Take out all
the words from the Ideas Bank 4 on page 237, for a start. This means that
simple objects (cat, dog, chair) and names (London, Gal Gadot, Manchester
United) are not allowed. Instead, you may choose one of the following types
of words to draw. I won't give you too many examples because if everybody
reads them, then they will be easy to guess.

- **Abstract nouns:** things, but not things you can touch, e.g., pride, success, love, or any word ending in -ment or -tion.

- **Verbs:** actions, e.g., running, crying, losing. (You can accept the guess in the *present participle* form—with the -ing ending—or the *infinitive* form, e.g., run, cry, lose.)

- **Adjectives:** words that describe a thing, e.g., muddy, ugly, exhausted.

- **Prepositions:** words that locate a thing, e.g., under, over, between.

You could, if you like, begin by telling the other players which type of word this is. Then begin to draw.

TIP

- Remember that it's difficult to see what someone's drawing if it's upside down or far away. Either everybody should sit on one side of a table, or you need to set up some sort of screen or easel, or mount some big paper on the wall so that everyone can see what you are doing. With lots of players, think about this well in advance of the game or it gets annoying.

NOW TRY THIS

- If some players brute-force a victory by yelling every word they know until they finally get it, you could limit each player to three guesses per round. Watch how they carefully wait until they're almost sure before guessing!

- You could extend the game to use well-known idioms or phrases, such as "Don't put the cart before the horse" or "Too many cooks spoil the broth."

84. The Exquisite Corpse

PLAYERS	DIFFICULTY	TIME
3+	Medium	20 mins

IN SHORT: Follow a sequence of word types to make
your own brand of nonsense.

TAGS:
GRAMMAR,
VOCABULARY,
SILLY,
COLLABORATIVE

WHAT YOU'LL NEED

• Paper and pencil for every player.

HOW TO PLAY

A game about grammar that's good for Christmas? But school's out! Nobody
wants an English lesson. Well . . . this one's a proper chuckler for every
generation. Give it a go.

Many sentences follow the same pattern of word classes. In other words,
we can generate sentences just by blindly following some simple rules. So,
we'll use this to make mischief.

Each player should write a **determiner** at the top of their piece of paper,
then fold the top over so that the next person cannot see it. Then everybody
passes their paper clockwise.

On the paper that you were passed, write an **adjective**, then fold it over.
The order of the words, which every person must use, is as follows:

• A **determiner** ("a," "an," or "the")

• An **adjective** (a descriptive word, like "sloppy")

• A **noun** (a thing, like "mailbox")

• A **verb** (an action, like "jumped")

• An **adverb** (describing a verb, like "politely")

• A **preposition** (positioning two nouns in relation to each other,
  like "under")

- A **possessive pronoun** (a word that shows ownership, like "his")

- Another **adjective** (a descriptive word, like "red")

- Another **noun** (a thing, like "spoon")

Once all nine words have been written on each piece of paper, it's time to unroll it and see the sentence that has been created!

Looking up at my list, I see that my sentence reads as follows: **The sloppy mailbox jumped politely under his red spoon.**

TIPS

- The more players the better. If there are only three (or fewer) of you playing, you might get too much say over what each particular sentence does.

- If your sentence doesn't make sense grammatically, feel free to add or alter a couple of words at the end of the game. For example, "a apple" might need changing to "an apple."

NOW TRY THIS

- Feeling bold? Use your random sentence as the first line for a story. See where it takes you.

85. Identity Crisis

PLAYERS	DIFFICULTY	TIME
4+	Medium	20 mins

IN SHORT: Work out who on earth you are, while helping others do the same.

TAGS: WIND-DOWN, GUESSING, CIRCLE GAMES

WHAT YOU'LL NEED

- Address labels or other stickers that will stay on a forehead. (I've seen people play this game with normal paper, a lick, and a prayer. If you're disgusting, like them, then go ahead.)

HOW TO PLAY

This game is a massive giggler, and perfect for bringing the family together because you're all working to help one another.

Every player must clearly write the name of a celebrity or fictional character on their sticker, then stick it on the forehead of the person on their left. It really helps if this character is well-known, particularly by the person who's about to have it stuck to them. You also need to make sure the person on your left doesn't see what you've written.

As soon as the sticker is on your forehead, everyone can see your "new name" except you. So, **it's your job to work out who you are!** Each player now takes turns asking the group a yes-or-no question about themselves, going around the circle. So, you might ask, "Am I real?" or "Am I famous for making something?"

If you think you know who you are, you may have a guess, but that will count as your turn. Once you have guessed correctly, then you may rip off your sticker (plus the top layer of your forehead skin), and spend the rest of the game just answering questions, not asking them.

TIPS

- Whatever your question, try to gain as much information as possible from the others' responses. For example, if Granny isn't answering your questions as much as other players, then perhaps you are better known by young people. If everybody laughs when you ask, "Do I have a special talent?," then perhaps you are somebody who has questionable skill at something, like Justin Bieber.

- This game doesn't work in a room with lots of mirrors, for obvious reasons! Similarly, don't let anybody go to the bathroom unless they've already guessed their name.

NOW TRY THIS

- Here's a fun ice-breaker for a party situation. Before your guests arrive, the host writes all the names on stickers, choosing related pairs of names (e.g., Mickey/Minnie, Barack/Michelle, Torvill/Dean) and then sticks them on the guests' foreheads as they come through the door. Rather than taking turns, each player may ask questions about themselves, but only one question to any one guest. So they'll be talking to as many people as possible, trying to work out who they are. However, the real aim is not only to work that out, but to find your pair. Once you and your pair think you've identified each other, link arms and ask another guest, "Are we a pair?" If so, you've won! Rip off those stickers and enjoy the rest of the party.

- If you play this version of the game, it's important that you never flat-out guess who you are. If you see "Prince Philip" and think you might be the pair, you may not ask somebody, "Am I Queen Elizabeth?" You could, however, ask, "Do I live in a palace?" or "Am I covered in corgis?"

86. Letter Links

PLAYERS	DIFFICULTY	TIME
2+	Medium	10–20 mins per chain

IN SHORT: Take turns to make a chain of related things, linked by letter.

TAGS: STRATEGY, MEMORY, SPELLING, WIND-DOWN

WHAT YOU'LL NEED

- Nothing at all.

HOW TO PLAY

A good circle game that dredges up all sorts of interesting ideas and memories from your turkey-plumped brains.

So, pick a nice broad category containing lots of members. You can find these on pages 251–52, or pick your own, but make sure it's a category that has hundreds of members. Musical artists or animals is a great start. Only pick a category within which everyone can name plenty of items. It's no fun if you pick baseball players and your mom doesn't like baseball.

One player should start by naming any member of that category. Rotate around the room clockwise, naming members of that category that **begin with the letter that ended the previous word**.

The game continues for as long as you can continue the chain. If somebody gets stuck, help them with clues, but don't give away an answer or it's just you having another turn.

EXAMPLE

The players have decided to name musical artists or bands. For bands that begin with "The," they skip this word.

Player 1: *"Beatles."*

(Player 1 has ended her answer on S. Player 2 must begin his with S.)

Player 2: *"Shirley Bassey."*

(Player 2 has ended his answer on Y. Player 3 must begin her answer with Y.)

Player 3: *"Yeah Yeah Yeahs."*

Etc.

TIP

- Quite quickly, you'll learn the danger letters. I've always played this as a team game, so ending your word with "x" is bad manners, really. If you want to be competitive, however, then it's a good ploy.

87. First Lines

PLAYERS	DIFFICULTY	TIME
4+	Medium	30 mins

IN SHORT: Can you fake the first line of a book?

WHAT YOU'LL NEED

TAGS: WRITING, CREATIVE, WIND-DOWN, CIRCLE GAMES

- Pencil and slips of paper for each person.

- A sheet of paper to keep score.

- A shelf full of books, preferably old or strange ones.

HOW TO PLAY

It's the day after Christmas. Your enormous extended family, cousins and uncles and aunts (oh my!), have all gathered at your granny's house, but there's nothing there but parquet floors, comfy chairs, and books. How on earth will you have a good time? This creative, cockle-warming game is all about mimicking the writing style of a book based on the cover and title. It's absurdly satisfying and, depending on who's playing, can be either hilarious and silly or a legitimate literary challenge.

Each round, one player becomes the librarian. They select a book from the bookshelf. It could be fiction or nonfiction, old or new, well-known or obscure.

Now the librarian displays the cover of the book for all of the other players. They could read the title aloud, show the cover image, and even recite some of the blurb. What they must **not** do is open the book up. Once everyone feels like they know what the book's about, it's time to play.

All of the players (except the librarian) must create what they think sounds convincingly like the first line of the book. You could decide together here whether you are going to write just the first line (ending in the middle of a sentence) or run on to the end of the first sentence. Both work great.

Write the line on a slip of paper and hand it to the librarian, making sure that nobody else sees it. Meanwhile, the librarian opens up the book to the first proper page (skipping over quotes, title page, and foreword, etc.) and writes down the real first line, adding this to the pile of fake first lines.

Once everybody has written a line, the librarian shuffles them up and reads them aloud. Everybody must listen carefully and decide which they think is the real line. At the end, each player except the librarian gets a guess.

- If you guess the correct first line, you get 1 point.

- If someone mistakes your fake first line for the real one, you get 1 point.

After the points have been added to the score sheet, the librarian should pass the job to the person on their left, and you can play another round! This time, try a completely different style of book.

EXAMPLE

The librarian picks out The Old Ways *by Robert Macfarlane.*

Librarian: *"The Old Ways: A Journey on Foot, by Robert Macfarlane. It's got a winding footpath on the front and a guy walking barefoot on the back. There's no blurb, I'm afraid."*

Player 1 *writes: "On a cool Thursday morning in February, I laced up my boots and set off for a walk that would change my life."*

Player 2 *writes: "When Tom Robertson lost his left foot in a terrible lawn-mowing accident, he thought he'd never walk again."*

Player 3 *submits: "I slept in a hedgerow that night, nestled among blackberries and their prickly twins, the thorns."*

The librarian *adds the real first line: "Two days short of the winter solstice; the turn of the year's tide."*

The librarian *shuffles the lines, then reads them aloud.* **Players 1** *and* **3** *vote for "Two days short . . ." and get a point each for a correct guess.* **Player 2** *votes for "On a cool . . . ," so* **Player 1** *gets another point for fooling somebody.*

Now Player 1 becomes the librarian, and he picks out Casper Candlewacks in Death by Pigeon, *by Ivan Brett. That sounds terrible.*

TIPS

- The librarian should read through the first lines in their head before reading them aloud, just to make sure that they don't struggle to read any handwriting, which would clearly give away which one was made up. Also, it might help them get any potential giggles out of the way.

- When writing, think about the age of the book, the style of language used in that type of book, the intended audience, and the content. They should all affect your first line.

NOW TRY THIS

- If you're in a group of people who like to be silly, the librarian can give special bonus points to the entry that earns the loudest laugh each round. This just means that people who had great ideas that weren't very convincing can still score points. It's best to award all these points before revealing who wrote each one, to avoid favoritism.

- How about flipping this around and having the players design the cover? Every player closes their eyes and the librarian picks out a book that they think nobody knows. Just from the title, every player has to sketch the cover, including image, text design, perhaps a quote. The closest to the real cover wins. (If you own the bookshelf, you might remember the cover, too, so for you to win, your cover will need to be *perfect*.)

88. Consequences

PLAYERS	DIFFICULTY	TIME
3+ . . . but the more the better!	Medium	10 mins per round

IN SHORT: The classic fold-over game where everybody's ideas mix around to make odd stories.

TAGS:
WRITING,
GRAMMAR,
COLLABORATIVE,
SILLY

WHAT YOU'LL NEED

- Lots of paper.

- Pencils for each player.

HOW TO PLAY

If you haven't played this with your family at Christmas, it's time to start. It's an oldie that I couldn't faithfully write a book of games without including. Every player starts with a piece of paper. Each round, they will write something, then fold the paper over so that their idea is hidden, and pass the paper to their left.

The whole idea of this game is that the stories end up being very silly indeed. So be creative about your words! Look in the examples for more help here.

The following is the order of what each person writes:

- An **adjective** that describes a person.

- A **man's name**.

- An **adjective** that describes a person.

- A **woman's name**.

- A **place**.

- An item of **clothing**.

- An item of **clothing**.

- A **sentence** to be spoken aloud.

- A **sentence** to be spoken aloud.

- The **consequence** (or what happened next).

- What the world said (a **general opinion**).

Now here's the fun part. Once each piece of paper has been written on, and folded over, eleven times, it is passed one final time and unrolled fully. Now players take turns reading out the story on the paper they've ended up holding using the following structure, but dropping in the words on your page in the right places:

One day, **1 2** met **3 4** at **5.** He wore **6.** She wore **7.** He said **8.** She said **9.** In the end, **10**, and the world said **11.**

EXAMPLE

*Once **Player 1** has unrolled her piece of paper, she reads the story, using all of the suggestions in order.*

"One day, wonky Steven met ten-feet-tall Emily on Mount Everest. He wore a pair of flying goggles. She wore a coat made of newspaper. He said, 'Pass the jelly.' She said, 'That's a very rude thing to say to a woman!' In the end, they started a band and toured the world. And the world said, 'No, thanks.'"

NOW TRY THIS

- There are only so many times to play this without it getting a little repetitive, but the game doesn't end there. Make up your own orders to create whole new stories. Use this one below, or create your own.
  1. Name
  2. Place
  3. Reason (because s/he . . .)
  4. An event (something happened)
  5. An event (something happened)
  6. A feeling or emotion

7. A verb (action—use past tense, e.g., "exploded" or "ate a banana")
8. Name
9. A verb (action—use present tense, e.g., "ride a unicyle" or "pick his nose")

1 went to **2** because s/he **3.** First of all, **4.** Then, **5.** After all that, s/he felt **6** so s/he **7.** In the end, **8** had to come and **9** to sort it all out.

89. Brian! Brian?

PLAYERS	DIFFICULTY	TIME
2+	Hard	5 mins +

IN SHORT: The weirdest method you'll ever use for counting to twenty.

TAGS:
NOISY, MATH,
ACTING, CODE

WHAT YOU'LL NEED

- Nothing at all.

HOW TO PLAY

Shake off the dead weight that was that extra portion of Christmas pudding by getting involved with this noisy, silly counting game.

I learned this one from a friend, Alice, and thought at first that she was kidding. It's full of performance and fun, and comes with a crack-up guarantee: if it doesn't make you laugh, I'll send you a replacement game.

Learning how to play takes a couple of stages, so bear with me.

Firstly, let's talk about Roman numerals. As I'm sure you know, the Romans used a combination of letters to stand for numbers. Here you will just need to be familiar with the numbers from 1 to 20:

1 = I	5 = V	9 = IX	13 = XIII	17 = XVII
2 = II	6 = VI	10 = X	14 = XIV	18 = XVIII
3 = III	7 = VII	11 = XI	15 = XV	19 = XIX
4 = IV	8 = VIII	12 = XII	16 = XVI	20 = XX

On we go to the next stage. We're going to replace each letter with a couple of words:

I = Brian!

V = Your friend Ian is here!

X = He wants to know if you can come out and play!

So, for example, the number 16 (XVI) would be, "He wants to know if you can come out and play! Your friend Ian is here! Brian!"

So, with this new code, you can count from 1 to 20 in a whole new way. In this game, players take turns saying the next number in the sequence, first translated into Roman numerals, then translated into Brian numerals.

But wait . . . there's more! The whole game should be performed as if you're an annoyed mother, calling upstairs to her son to alert him of a visitor at the door. When I was told this game, the mother was also Australian. I don't know how important that aspect is, but if you've come this far, you may as well go with that extra complication.

Take your string of motherly nags and *really* act it. You could join sentences, change emphasis, or anything, really, except change the words or order.

Rather than being competitive, if somebody goes wrong or gets confused, give them a hand remembering the order and then let them have a crack at it again. It shouldn't be a mean game, especially when acting is required.

EXAMPLE

Player 1: *"Brian!"*
Player 2: *"Brian! Brian?"*
Player 3: *"Brian! Brian? Brian!"*
Player 4: *"Brian? Your friend Ian is here!"*
Player 1: *"Your friend Ian is here!"*
Player 2: *"Your friend Ian is here, Brian!"*
Etc.

NOW TRY THIS

- If you need more, then here it is. Look at the game **Twenty-One Dares** in this very book (page 42). The game can be played not with numbers but with Brians, for total confusion for anybody listening in.

- Or, if you don't want to turn it into a dares game, just keep counting. How about 50 (L) being "He's still waiting!" and 100 (C) being "For God's sake!" Now 162 would be "For God's sake! He's still waiting! He wants to know if you can come out and play! Brian! Brian?"

90. Blabbermouth

PLAYERS	DIFFICULTY	TIME
3+	**Hard**	**20-40 mins**

IN SHORT: A take on the classic talking game, which forces you to think on your feet.

TAGS:
CREATIVE,
MEMORY,
STRATEGY,
COMPETITIVE

WHAT YOU'LL NEED

- A stopwatch that can count down. Almost every smartphone has this function.

- Talking topics (pages 229–30) printed out or photocopied, then cut out and put into a hat.

- Invisible buzzers, one for each person. (You could use a bell or a kazoo, or anything noisy, but personally, I'm a big fan of creating my own invisible one. Not only is it free, but you can also spend multiple hours honing your own personal noise. I do a kind of honk while pressing downward with my fingers knitted together, but don't let that sway you.)

- Paper and pencil, to keep score.

HOW TO PLAY

This old favorite gives everyone a chance to have a chat, and it's perfect when you have different generations sitting together. Choose one player to be the judge. This will change after every round, so don't fret about who goes first. The player directly to the judge's right, the speaker, picks a **talking topic** from the hat. She reads it aloud to the other players, and then the judge *immediately* begins the countdown timer.

The speaker has to speak for one minute on the topic in hand. However, there are rules. Any other player (except the judge) may buzz the speaker if she breaks one of these three rules:

- **Pausing:** The big one. You cannot stop to think. Any pause longer than a hurried breath is punishable by a buzz.

- **Going off topic:** If your subject is "Bees," and you talk about honey, and then honey on toast, and then beans on toast, that's off topic. (If you talked about bees on toast, then that would be fine. Also delicious.) Another example of going off topic is speaking in nonsense or just counting, for example.

- **Repeating a word:** This is a tricky one. For experts, you should not be allowed to repeat any word except for the ones on the card. For beginners, repetition of high-frequency words such as "the," "but," and "I" could be allowed. Make sure that you agree on the rule *before you begin*, to avoid arguments. (And don't try repeating the words on the card again and again. That's mega-cheating.)

As soon as another player buzzes in, then the judge stops the timer. The player explains which rule has been broken, and if the judge agrees, then the buzzing-in player gets a point, as well as becoming the new speaker. The timer restarts with whatever time is left and the new player must talk about the same subject. If the buzz-in was wrong, then the speaker gets a point and is allowed to carry on.

Whoever is the speaker when the time runs out is rewarded with an extra point. The judge passes the stopwatch to the player on their left, and the player who *was* the judge now picks a new card.

EXAMPLE

Player 1 picks the subject "Roller Skates." The judge begins the timer and calls, "Go."

Player 1: *"I hate roller skates because I always fall over. I always go too fast and then—"*

Player 2: *"HONK! Repetition of 'always.'"*

Judge: *"Yes, correct. Player 2, you get a point and have 55 seconds. Go."*

Player 2: *"I've always been better on a skateboard than roller skates. They have more wheels and you can do tricks."*

Player 3: *"BEEP! Off topic. She's talking about skateboards."*

Judge: *"Yes she is. Player 3, you get a point and have 48 seconds remaining. Go."*

Player 3: *"I used to go with my brother to roller-skate around the multi-story parking garage. One day we—"*

Player 2: *"HONK! He stopped."*

Judge: *"No, he was just taking a breath between sentences. Player 3 gets a point and continues with 41 seconds. Go!"*

Etc.

TIP

- This game is all about improvising under pressure. If the fear of being buzzed is freezing one of the players up entirely, be more generous with the rules and just let your opponent talk for a while. You could even remove the buzzing altogether and give the player a minute to talk however they like. You could discuss how they did afterward. This is just as much fun, but altogether less stressful.

CHAPTER 10
JUST CHILL OUT

It's been a tough day. It started when you opened the fridge too hard and the orange juice toppled out. Even after you'd mopped up the explosion, you had sticky footsteps all day and had to change your trousers. Weather-wise, it was the sort of rain that doesn't seem bad enough for an umbrella until you've been out in it for ten minutes and realize you look like a soggy water vole. You had made a vital to-do list at work, but an unwanted 9:00 a.m. email meant you spent the whole day on the phone with the IT person, trying to reroute the UDI credentials, or something. And worst of all, your lunch leaked in your bag, so everything you own now has the color and scent of balsamic vinegar. By the time you get home, you just need someone to look after you, but your other half comes through the door even grumpier than you.

You need to chill out.

And I have just the set of games for that!

It may not feel like games are quite the solution right now, but these will heal a frazzled brain with their soothing, low-intensity nature and ability to take your mind off the world's stresses. Here are word games, alphabet challenges, and streams-of-consciousness that will wipe clear your mind and relax you right down.

They are also great games for helping kids (or overexcitable adults) keep chilled and calm in any situation. Perhaps you're expecting an important phone call and need a bit of peace, or you want an alternative to family movies on TV one lazy afternoon.

I've even thrown in a couple of insanely inspiring writing games, for those who relax by getting a little creative.

91. Word Association

PLAYERS	DIFFICULTY	TIME
2+	Easy	5 mins

IN SHORT: A stream-of-consciousness back-and-forth game.

TAGS:
VOCABULARY,
CREATIVE,
WIND-DOWN

WHAT YOU'LL NEED

• Nothing at all.

HOW TO PLAY

One player starts with a word—any word—and says it to the group. Working clockwise, the players have to come up with a synonym (a word that means the same thing) or really any word that's linked in some way. The entertaining part is to see where the trail leads, and how much the meaning can change over time. Words with double meanings, or "homonyms" ("fair," for example), are particularly useful because you can change direction so suddenly.

EXAMPLE

Player 1: "Blue."
Player 2: "Sky."
Player 3: "Television."
Player 4: "Film."
Player 1: "Camera."
Etc.

NOW TRY THIS

• In Word Association you have to use words that have some relation to the previous one. In Word *Disassociation*, you have to choose a word that has **absolutely no relation** to the previous word.

- The really fun part comes when you challenge other players. If you see a relationship between the words that the others didn't, then you can force them to think of another word.

EXAMPLE

Player 1: *"Egg."*
Player 2: *"Chelsea."*
Player 3: *"Green."*
Player 4: *"Sandal."*
Player 1: *"Mayonnaise."*
Player 2: *"Seagull."*
Player 4: *"Challenge! They're both white!"*
Player 2: *"Okay, then. Thursday."*
Etc.

TIP

- There are many ways for words to associate. They could rhyme, start with the same letter (alliteration), or any number of other things. Most words could probably be associated with each other, so try to find that link!

92. Why?

PLAYERS	DIFFICULTY	TIME
2	Medium	10 mins

IN SHORT: Why?

TAGS:
STRATEGY,
CONVERSATION,
CREATIVE

WHAT YOU'LL NEED

- Nothing at all.

HOW TO PLAY

WARNING: This game can become intensely annoying if you're not playing. It is, however, great for pushing further and further into the reasons why things are the way they are. But be aware of others. If they are getting annoyed, choose another game.

One player, the explainer, begins by making a statement.

The other, the questioner, asks, "Why?"

The explainer answers the best she can.

The questioner asks, "Why?"

The game continues for as long as possible. The explainer should try not to repeat herself, or use answers like "It just is." Try to *really* think why something is the way it is.

Once you get stuck, switch roles and begin with a new statement.

EXAMPLE

Explainer: "My lasagna is taking ages to arrive."
Questioner: "Why?"
Explainer: "Because it takes a long time to cook."
Questioner: "Why?"
Explainer: "Because it has to go in the oven."
Questioner: "Why?"
Explainer: "Because if you cooked it in a saucepan, it would get all mashed up."

Questioner: *"Why?"*

Explainer: *"Because you'd have to stir it."*

Questioner: *"Why?"*

Explainer: *"Or else it would burn on the bottom."*

Questioner: *"Why?"*

Explainer: *"Because when you use a saucepan, the heat comes from below the pan."*

Questioner: *"Why?"*

Explainer: *"Because that's how stoves work."*

Questioner: *"Why?"*

Explainer: *"Because somebody designed it like that."*

Questioner: *"Why?"*

Explainer: *"Because they'd seen people cook over fires, and this is similar."*

Etc.

93. Fit-It

PLAYERS	DIFFICULTY	TIME
2	Medium	20 mins

IN SHORT: A bit like Hangman, but far more interesting.

TAGS: SPELLING, GUESSING, COMPETITIVE, STRATEGY

WHAT YOU'LL NEED

- Whiteboard and dry-erase markers, or pencil and paper.

HOW TO PLAY

I created this game when trying to think of a more interesting alternative to Hangman to use in class. The aim was to encourage children to think of a word differently, as a combination of prefixes, roots, and suffixes, and to ask questions like "What sort of word has a G as the final letter?" If that all sounds a bit too schooly, swallow that thought, then just try. It's a fun little two-player game no matter what.

The aim of the game is to **guess a secret word**. One player, the leader, thinks it up in their head (no names or slang: the usual rules), then at the top of the page draws a horizontal dotted line, one line for each letter, just like the start of a Hangman round.

However, this is where the two games diverge. The guesser must guess the **entire word**, not a letter. The aim is for the word to "fit." So at this stage, it's easy: the guessed word must be simply the right length. The guesser writes their guess down, and as long as it fits, they score 1 point.

Unless they're incredibly lucky or can read minds, they probably got it wrong, so now the leader fills in one letter of the mystery word at the top of the page. It could be any of the letters in the word, but make sure it's in the right place!

The guesser must again write a word that fits, both in length and now taking into account the letter that they know. Once again, they get a point as long as their guess fits.

If, at any point, the guesser simply cannot think of a word that fits, then they can pass. They will get no points for that guess, but earn another letter in the word to help with the next one.

This carries on, with the leader giving away an extra letter with every incorrect guess, until the guesser correctly finds the word. At this point they get 2 points for every empty letter still in the word. Then the score is tallied up, and the players swap for another word of *the same length*, so that it's fair.

EXAMPLE

Leader *has chosen the word SALMON. She writes* _ _ _ _ _ _ *at the top of the page.*

Guesser *guesses JUMPED. It's wrong, but it fits, so she gets 1 point.*

Leader *gives away one mystery letter. The word at the top now reads _ _ L _ _ _.*

Guesser *guesses PILLAR. It's wrong, but it fits with the L, so she gets 1 point.*

Leader *gives away another letter. _ _ L _ O _.*

Guesser *tries to guess BALOON, but that's not how you spell it. Instead,* **Guesser** *guesses BALLOT. It's wrong, but it fits, so she gets 1 point.*

Leader *gives away another letter. _ _ L _ O N.*

Guesser *tries to guess BOLTON, but that's a name. She passes, for 0 points.*

Leader *gives away another letter. S _ L _ O N.*

Guesser *guesses SALMON, giving her 4 points (2 for each letter that was still unknown). Overall, she scored 7 points.*

TIP

- To master this game, you must think about prefixes and suffixes. These are sets of letters that affix to the front and back (respectively) of a word, changing its meaning or function. For example, the *ful* of wonderful and the *im* of impossible. Once you're looking for these, you'll be able to use clues to fit more letters around the ones that you know. So if a word ends in G, it's likely to end in ING, because that's a really common suffix.

94. A–Z of . . .

PLAYERS	DIFFICULTY	TIME
1+	Medium	10 mins per alphabet

IN SHORT: A to-and-fro alphabet game.

WHAT YOU'LL NEED

* Nothing at all.

TAGS: CREATIVE, SPELLING, COLLABORATIVE, PASS THE TIME

HOW TO PLAY

The aim of the game is to complete an alphabet of a certain category. You'll take turns thinking of **26** things within that category and call them out, and if you make it to the end of the alphabet, you all win.

Pick a category from pages 251–52, or make up your own. Remember, some categories are easier than others.

You could write your answers down on paper, but there's no need. If a player gets stuck, she can ask for help if she needs it. If you want to make it competitive, give each player a time limit and if they can't think of an answer within the time, they're buzzed OUT. (In truth, this game is better if you work as a team, but some people love a competition.)

EXAMPLE

The players choose A–Z of chunky things.
Player 1: *"Apple."*
Player 2: *"Brick."*
Player 3: *"Chocolate chunks."*
Player 1: *"Doughnut."*
Etc.

TIPS

- Don't get too stuck on whether an answer is right or wrong. Even if it doesn't quite fit (like "Orange" in your A–Z of Red Things), just accept it and move on.

- Here's a secret: I actually use this game to go to sleep almost every night. Pick a really tough subject and experience your mind wandering to odd, sleepy places trying to find a sticky thing beginning with C. (Chewing gum. Took me ages!) You'll be asleep before you know it.

- Another way to play this game is to write the alphabet on a piece of paper or whiteboard, and the category at the top. Then try, as quickly as you can, to cross off each letter by shouting a word in that category. You can do this in any order, so it becomes a scramble to get off the easy ones and then seek out the more difficult letters. You'll need someone to adjudicate to make sure your answers all qualify—why not ask them to time you, too, so you can try to set a world record? Then you can challenge yourself to beat it with a different category.

- For a competitive written version of this game, try **Category Scramble** (see page 159).

95. Word Ladders

PLAYERS	DIFFICULTY	TIME
1+	Medium	15 mins

IN SHORT: Change a letter, change a letter, change a letter. How far can you go?

TAGS:
SPELLING,
VOCABULARY,
STRATEGY,
WIND-DOWN

WHAT YOU'LL NEED

• Pencil and paper (or mini whiteboard and dry-erase markers).

HOW TO PLAY

One player writes a four-letter word on the whiteboard. The second player is allowed to swap one letter for another, and write a new word below it. This goes on for as long as you can, replacing just one letter each time. No repeated words, names, or slang!

EXAMPLE

TURN
BURN
BARN
BARK
BANK
BUNK
BUCK
BULK

TIPS

• If you find this hard, write out the alphabet and use it to help you.

• Part of what makes this hard is not even knowing which letter to swap out. If you're playing with somebody who needs some support, try to think of a valid word in your head and then write out the three letters that stay the same. The other player simply has to find the missing letter, knowing that there will be an answer. For example, after "SAND" you could write "AND," after which he might find "HAND."

NOW TRY THIS

- If this game is too easy, pick one four-letter word to start with and one to end on, and try to get between them in as few steps as possible. This can be furiously difficult, but definitely worth a try. Can you make a ladder from BLACK to WHITE? DOG to CAT? DAWN to DUSK?

- A tip for this version of the game is to try to get vowels and consonants in the right place before you worry about the particular letters.

96. Right on Target

PLAYERS	DIFFICULTY	TIME
2+	**Hard**	**Ongoing**

IN SHORT: Reach a number between 1 and 1,000 as fast as you can.

TAGS:
MATH,
COMPETITIVE,
STRATEGY

WHAT YOU'LL NEED

• Whiteboard and dry-erase markers, or pencil and paper for each player.

HOW TO PLAY

This simple math challenge is difficult at first, but great practice for keeping that brain of yours fizzing along. Also, if you're competitive, it's great for racing.

At the top of your page or board, choose five digits between **1** and **9**, and the number **100**. These will be your tools: the numbers you'll use to get to the target.

Next, it's time to pick the target. Search online for a random number generator. There are loads. Otherwise, pluck a number out of thin air. Either way, it should be somewhere between 1 and 1,000.

As soon as all the players have the tools and the target, it's time to begin. Add, subtract, multiply, and divide your way to the target. **You don't have to use all of the numbers, but you cannot use any number twice.**

You could do this part in a number of ways. Either give yourself a time limit—say, two minutes—to get the answer, or stop the clock as soon as the first player gets it. Then it's time to put down your pencils and share results. You may only score points based on what's on your whiteboard/page, to avoid copying, so write down your method clearly.

If you hit the target, you get 10 points. Then it's 9 points if you were 1 off, 8 if you were 2 off, and so on.

Keep on playing to build your score. First to 100 points wins!

EXAMPLE

The players choose the numbers 2, 3, 5, 6, 9, and 100. The random target is 541. After two minutes, they share results.

Player 1: "5 x 100 is 500. Then add that to 9 x 6, which is 54. 554 − 3 then −2 is 549." *(549 is 8 from the target so scores 2 points.)*

Player 2: "5 x 100, that's all I got." *(500 is too far away. Player 2 scores 0 points.)*

Player 3: "6 x 100 = 600, then do 5 + 2, multiply that by 9, that's 63. Take away 3 makes 60. 600 − 60 is 540." *(540 scores 9 points.)*

TIPS

- The simplest tactic is to shoot for the right number of hundreds and adjust from there, but take care that you're getting as close as possible. For example, if your target was 786, you might try to reach 700, but 800 is actually much closer, if you can get there.

- Remember that you can adjust the numbers before multiplying by 100. If you have 7, 2, and 100, and want to get to 900, add the 7 and 2 first.

- If you really are stuck, work backward from the target. Sometimes that helps.

NOW TRY THIS

- The TV show *Countdown* has a similar game, but there are more options with your starting numbers: 100 is replaced by 25, 50, 75, or 100 and you can choose to have another of those in place of one of your digits. Also, they have big cards and a massive clock. Even if you can't find a massive clock, the rest is still available to you with a bit of printing and cutting.

- It's really worthwhile trying to put your entire method into one number sentence, using brackets to keep the calculations in the right order. For help on brackets, ask a child, because they've been to school more recently than you!

97. Ten-to-One Story

PLAYERS	DIFFICULTY	TIME
1+	Hard	20-30 mins

IN SHORT: A short-story writing challenge with one simple, yet tricky, rule.

TAGS: CREATIVE, WRITING, VOCABULARY, WIND-DOWN

WHAT YOU'LL NEED

• List of story titles (see pages 243–45).

• Paper and pencil.

HOW TO PLAY

Your challenge is to write a story using one of the story prompts. However, it may have only ten sentences. The first sentence must have exactly ten words. The second must have nine, the third must have eight, and so on, until the final sentence has only one word. This game forces you to be aware of the words that you use, and the impact of each one.

You could put each sentence in its own paragraph, like I have done, or put them all together into one block of text. Set it out however you like.

If you have spare ink in your pen, you could do the same but with twenty-to-one.

Good luck!

EXAMPLE

I used the story prompt "My Last Day on Earth."

"Ten, Nine, Eight," began Mission Control, and the engine roared.
I held my breath until the voice reached zero.
The force was intense: gravity wanted me back.
Finally, I was leaving all life behind.
Now I floated alone in space.

The eternal darkness embraced me.
Then I saw them.
The moon's eyes.
Waking up.
Hungry.

TIPS

- There's no single way to play this game, and the best way would just be to start and see what happens. BUT, if you want your story to have a knockout ending, think about the last word first. It's alone in its own sentence. Make that word have real clout. Could it be a twist? A cliffhanger?

- Try to vary the structure of your sentences and avoid repetition. I've played this game with people who cop out with stories such as "Fuzzy bunny wanted to eat a delicious, yummy, orange carrot. Fuzzy bunny went to the carrot shop for one. Fuzzy bunny bought a carrot and ate one." Seriously, stop that.

98. Grow a Word

PLAYERS	DIFFICULTY	TIME
1+	Hard	20 mins

IN SHORT: Teamwork game where you add and jumble letters to make a word as large as possible.

TAGS:
SPELLING,
VOCABULARY,
STRATEGY

WHAT YOU'LL NEED

• Pencil and paper (or mini whiteboard and dry-erase markers).

HOW TO PLAY

Work as a team for this game. Here's how it plays:

Start with a **two-letter word**. (No names or abbreviations.) The challenge is now to add one letter, any that you like, and form a new three-letter word. You are also allowed to jumble the letters that you already have.

Continue adding one letter and jumbling the existing letters, if needed, to make new words. How far can you get? It's possible, with time and effort, to grow enormous words from the tiniest of seeds.

EXAMPLE

TO
TOE
NOTE
TONER
MENTOR
TORMENT
TORMENTS
(. . . and that's as far as I got. Can you go further?)

TIP

- Anagrams are hard. On a piece of paper or a whiteboard, write your letters randomly in a cloud shape and play around with them. Look for common letter blends such as "sh" or "-ing."

NOW TRY THIS

- If you get stuck, you could agree that taking away a letter is permitted as a move, as long as you don't return to the same word as before. In that way, you could work laterally to get to the biggest word possible, even if it takes you a few failed attempts.

99. Write Against the Odds

PLAYERS	DIFFICULTY	TIME
1+	Hard	45 mins

IN SHORT: A bunch of ideas that make writing stupidly hard, but stupidly fun.

TAGS: CREATIVE, WRITING, WIND-DOWN

WHAT YOU'LL NEED

- Lists of story titles (pages 243–45) or first lines (pages 246–50).

- Paper and pencil.

HOW TO PLAY

In a similar way to **Ten-to-One Story** (see page 220), giving yourself a weird limit on how you are allowed to write should force you to be creative in a number of new and interesting ways. Try it! Here are a few limitations you can place on your own writing. Choose one or more (not all of them!), pick a story prompt, and begin:

- Pick a letter. You may not use this letter anywhere in your story.

- Your story must be *exactly* 101 words long.

- You have five minutes to write your story. Do not stop writing, or look up from the page, until the five minutes are up, even if that means writing nonsense. (This is also called a "splurge.")

- Spell every word wrong.

- You may not use the same word twice.

- Start at the bottom of the page. Write the final sentence, then the penultimate sentence, and so on until you write the first sentence.

- Every character is called David.

- You may write only when your eyes are closed.

- Write the whole thing with your wrong hand.

- Your whole story is one long sentence. No periods and lots of conjunctions!

- Hold your breath. Every time you breathe as you write the story, draw a spiral over the word you just wrote.

- Every word must contain three letters.

- Pick a letter. Every word must contain that letter.

100. Talk Like Shakespeare

PLAYERS	DIFFICULTY	TIME
1+	Hard	**Learn in 10 mins, practice for life**

IN SHORT: Learn about the glories of iambic pentameter, then spend your life using it.

TAGS: CONVERSATION, VOCABULARY, GRAMMAR, PASS THE TIME, LONG-TERM

WHAT YOU'LL NEED

- Nothing at all.

HOW TO PLAY

You may be a Shakespeare fan or totally put off by his dense language, but either way, you have to admit that there's something special about the way that he writes.

Well, part of it is the rhythm. You see, Shakespeare writes almost entirely in iambic pentameter. That is, every line has exactly five groups of two syllables (so ten overall), and in each pair, the second is more stressed than the first.

So, in plain English, a line of Shakespeare's verse should sound like this: Da DUM da DUM da DUM da DUM da DUM.

It has a certain pace to it, and a flow. When you read Shakespeare in full knowledge of iambic pentameter, it actually reads better. Try reading this extract from the prologue to *Romeo and Juliet* aloud:

> *Two households, both alike in dignity,*
> *In fair Verona, where we lay our scene,*
> *From ancient grudge break to new mutiny,*
> *Where civil blood makes civil hands unclean.*

Anyway, here's where you come in. See if you can speak in iambic pentameter. Have a feel for which words and phrases work best. And most of all, prance about the place as if you're in Elizabethan times while you do it. You could even wear a ruff.

EXAMPLE

Player 1: *"I really want a piece of toast with jam."*

Player 2: *"Then go ahead and make one, greedy guts."*

Player 1: *"But my poor head is aching, and I'm tired."*

Player 2: *"I'm not your slave; get your own stupid toast."*

Ideas Bank 1:

TALKING TOPICS

Specifically for use in **Blabbermouth** (page 203), this is a set of cards to pick from a hat, each giving you something to talk about for one minute. Of course, feel free to make your own, too.

My favorite holiday	How to bake a cake
The world's worst job	If I ruled the world
My biggest secret	Sandcastles
The neighbors	Halloween
My proudest achievement	Wolves
The human brain	Water slides
Knitting	The best season
Chili peppers	The guitar
The city where I live	Treehouses
Broken bones	The Internet
Strange pets	Supermarkets
Hottest day of the year	Chores

Playing the piano	How to draw a horse
Dreams	Rhubarb
Video games	Chocolate
Cliffs	Bicycles
Thursdays	Cousins
If I were a cat	Ten years' time
Fruit vs. vegetables	Superman vs. Batman
Girls vs. boys	My perfect burger
The panda	The United States of America
Vegetarianism	Magic tricks
Spiders	How does digestion work?
Airplanes	My claim to fame
How I got this scar	The best meal I can cook
Ads on TV	Rock climbing

Ideas Bank 2:

STORY INGREDIENTS—CHARACTER

For various games in this book you will need some random story ingredients. Photocopy these pages or just copy them out if you have a spare minute, cut them up, and keep them separate from the other categories, in bags. Pick one out every time you need a new **character**.

King	Princess
President	Homeless person
Queen	Prince
Acrobat	Model
Athlete	Hacker
Vampire	Werewolf
Scientist	Doctor
Gardener	Soldier
Pilot	Schoolchild
Teacher	Criminal
Old man	Old woman
Police officer	Runaway
Explorer	Firefighter
Teenager	Soccer player
Artist	Singer

Vandal	Spy
Truck driver	Ninja
Bully	Clown
Rich person	Servant
Con man	Ghost
Refugee	Hunter
Detective	Guard
Knight	Pirate
Astronaut	Alien
Chef	Rock climber
Bus driver	Hiker
Sailor	Fire-breather
Thief	Pickpocket
Gangster	Superhero
Bodybuilder	Wrestler
Zombie	Giant
Baby	Fashion designer
Diver	Skydiver
Cleaner	Preacher
Musician	Salesperson

Street performer	Mugger
Thug	Ballerina
Dancer	Farmer
Plastic surgeon	Garbage collector
Camper	Motorcyclist
Shop assistant	Genius
Hypnotist	TV presenter
News anchor	Bird-watcher
Fisherman	Hairdresser

Ideas Bank 3:

STORY INGREDIENTS—PLACE

For various games in this book you will need some random story ingredients. Photocopy these pages or just copy them out if you have a spare minute, cut them up, and keep them separate from the other categories, in bags. Pick one out every time you need a new **place**.

Main street	**Bus stop**
Up a tree	**Cliff top**
On a stage	**Zoo**
Supermarket	**Clothing shop**
Restaurant	**Alleyway**
Train station	**Airport**
By a river	**On a roof**
Train	**Jungle**
Woodland	**Stadium**
School	**TV studio**
Aboard a ship	**The Arctic**
Desert	**Park**
Swimming pool	**Cinema**
Hospital	**Mountain**
Highway	**Prison**

Beach	Barbershop
Graveyard	Mansion
Castle	Factory
Basement	Dungeon
Spaceship	Casino
Circus	Art gallery
Theme park	Police station
At home	Rock concert
Battlefield	Wedding
Birthday party	Church
Summer fair	Festival
Campsite	Vacation resort
Penthouse	Garden
The moon	A very long line
Furniture shop	Coal mine
Playground	Swamp
Pyramid	Hotel
Café	Underwater
Elevator	Bookshop
Market	Maze

Farm	Bank
Ski slope	Log cabin
Ruins	Desert island
Tiny boat	Soccer field
Building site	Backstage
Haunted house	Walk-in freezer
Laundromat	Garbage dump
Parking garage	Skyscraper
Belly of a whale	Skate park

Ideas Bank 4:

STORY INGREDIENTS—OBJECT

For various games in this book you will need some random story ingredients. Photocopy these pages or just copy them out if you have a spare minute, cut them up, and keep them separate from the other categories, in bags. Pick one out every time you need a new **object**.

Mysterious box	**Scissors**
Coin	**Hose**
Flower	**Poison**
Letter	**Suitcase**
Seed	**Hamburger**
Cup	**Cat**
Computer	**Tablet**
Toy	**Telephone**
Spider	**Sock**
Towel	**Rubber band**
Hat	**Fake mustache**
Glasses	**Tie**
Shoes	**Butter**
Swimming trunks	**Needle**
Bucket of water	**Fish**

Drone	Ball
Trophy	Medal
Key	Watch
Rock	String
Poster	Newspaper
Cushion	Bird
Cucumber	Rat
Lightbulb	Test tube
DVD	Pen
Paint	Ironing board
Walkie-talkie	Headphones
Mask	Chocolate bar
Hot-water bottle	Map
Lunch box	Handcuffs
Helmet	Wellington boots
Cup of tea	Guitar
Trumpet	Crown
Coat hanger	Walking stick
Horseshoe	Pad of paper
Wooden spoon	Champagne glass

Teapot	Spade
Joystick	Skateboard
Scooter	Bicycle
Book	Guinea pig
Paper clip	Tooth
Snorkel	Compass
Jewel	Ring
Magnifying glass	Jam
Magnet	Pickax

Ideas Bank 5:

STORY INGREDIENTS—ACTION

For various games in this book you will need some random story ingredients. Photocopy these pages or just copy them out if you have a spare minute, cut them up, and keep them separate from the other categories, in bags. Pick one out every time you need a new **action**.

An argument	An agreement
A lie	A secret
An apology	A message
A plea	A promise
A betrayal	A theft
Something is found	A loss
A purchase	A sale
An order	A law is broken
A quest	An adventure
A journey	A gasp
Somebody runs	A fall
A climb	A mistake
Confusion	Something grows
Something shrinks	Somebody sleeps
A victory	A defeat

A death	An injury
Something heals	A trial
A trick	A fight
A chase	Something is caught
A race	A game
A leap	A meeting
A search	Something is built
Something is destroyed	A plan
Something is written	A laugh
Something is burned	Somebody cries
A wish	A slip
A fright	Somebody tiptoes
Somebody hides	A decision
Something is drawn	A swim
A dream	A gift
Somebody fails	A collapse
A lick	A scream
A whisper	Something flies
A secret meeting	A choice

Something gets wet	A phone call
Something stinks	A taste
A reveal	A rush
Something freezes	Something rolls
A handshake	A high five
A U-turn	A screech
A panic	A scratch
Somebody digs	A flip
Something is opened	A held breath
Something is closed	A thump

Ideas Bank 6:

100 STORY TITLES

These are needed for **Ten-to-One Story** (page 220) and **Write Against the Odds** (page 224), but they're a useful resource more generally.

A fellow writer and friend was astonished and appalled that I'd give away 100 free titles, with the opinion that I'd run out of them to use for my own books. Well, if that happens, then at least you'll have some for yours. Take any one, write it at the top of your paper, and get writing.

If you want to make this a little crazy, search online for a random number generator. Set the maximum number to "100" and press "generate." Whatever number comes up, pick that title and go.

If your stories are normally too long, or you never finish them, give yourself a time limit. If they're always too short, set a page target to achieve. Good luck!

100 TITLES	
1. Curse	15. Sea Rising
2. The Day That Lasted a Year	16. Rivals
3. Pathetic Peter	17. Grandmother's Rug
4. Nobody Leaves Until . . .	18. Night of the Wasps
5. Broken	19. ENTER PASSWORD
6. Spaghetti Massacre	20. Girl with a Red Hood
7. Calm Before the Storm	21. Ten in a Broken Elevator
8. Mirror World	22. No Parachute
9. My Iron Eyes	23. Meal of Worms
10. Greed	24. There Is No London
11. The Longest Journey	25. The Missing Dagger
12. Takeoff!	26. How Many Cats Is Too Many Cats?
13. Last Train South	
14. Behind the Walls	27. Five Percent Battery

28. Alone
29. Bridge
30. Death of the Sun
31. Hell Has Free Parking
32. Last Breath
33. Simon's Claws
34. Down the Drain
35. Revenge of the Bananas
36. My Undead Family
37. The Crying Wall
38. Worst Birthday Ever
39. The Man Who Climbed a Tree and Never Came Down
40. Jealous of You
41. Stopped Clocks
42. Under My Feet
43. World Record
44. It's Always Night in Space
45. Let Sleeping Dogs Lie
46. Friend Factory
47. Hat Glue
48. No More Teachers
49. The Bird Magnet
50. Poison Jam
51. I Planted a Spoon
52. Chocolate Dreams
53. Man on Your Roof
54. Downhill Race
55. One Character in This Story Is a Murderer
56. Everybody Knows Your Secret
57. No Way Out
58. Allergic to Air
59. Last Boy on Earth
60. Tooth Thief
61. One Roll of the Dice
62. Nobody Knows My *Real* Real Name
63. A Second Me
64. A Day in the Fridge
65. Pocket Elephant
66. Sky Pirate
67. Final Challenge
68. Hidden Inside
69. One Hundred Degrees
70. Nobody Believes Me
71. Happy Death Day
72. Top of the Clock Tower
73. Somebody Spat on Me
74. Walking Through Walls
75. Mushroom City
76. Storm Clouds
77. Copycat
78. Just STOP Growing!
79. George and the Dark Place
80. One New Message

81. Second-Best Treehouse
82. I'm Not Pretending
83. Old Smugglers' Road
84. My Best Friend, the Whale
85. Craig Collects Coins
86. Angel Trap
87. Lightning Shop
88. Around the World in Eighty Hours
89. Stuck on the Subway
90. What's Over the Horizon?
91. Noah's Ark 2
92. The First Word Ever Spoken
93. Science Class Will Never End
94. Bent Steel
95. A Story Without Words
96. Pest Control
97. Plague
98. Picnic on the Highway
99. Never Touch the Ground
100. Fortune-Teller

Ideas Bank 7:

100 OPENING LINES

These are needed for **Endless Sentence** (page 113), **Ten-to-One Story** (page 220), and **Write Against the Odds** (page 224), but they're a useful resource more generally.

The hardest part of a story is the first line. So, since I'm so kind, I've done the hard part for you! Below are more opening lines than you'll ever need. Take any one, write it on the first line of your paper, and get writing.

1. The beast had stopped snoring. That could mean only one thing . . .

2. My mom looked different this morning. All through breakfast I couldn't place what had changed.

3. My name is Albert, and I am dead.

4. Usually, there's a portrait on my wall of a boy and his dog. Today, there's just a dog.

5. The woods were dark and deep, but a distant light shone, far ahead.

6. Harry was probably the first person you've ever met with a pet tiger.

7. "Sleep well," said Dad, and he closed the door. But I wouldn't sleep. Not tonight.

8. As the countdown reached zero, the crowd roared. It had begun.

9. She had been hiding on this train for three days so far.

10. "Roll up, roll up!" announced the ringmaster. "Step inside my house of horrors!"

11. Fifty-five burgers sat on the table in front of him.

12. I began to shrink at lunchtime.

13. On her three thousandth birthday, Zoe had an idea.

14. "Come with me if you want to live," said the huge man.

15. How far underground was I now?

16. I think I'm the only human in this classroom.

17. "You're grounded!" shouted Mom. "For a year!"

18. When Dave awoke, he had the strangest feeling that he was sinking.

19. "Water," I gasped. "I need water!"

20. I didn't know my pizza was magic until I had finished the final slice.

21. It started as a sore throat. Then, Sasha had a cough.

22. The curtain rose; the audience fell silent. This was my moment.

23. From inside the suitcase came a soft ticking noise.

24. "It is finished!" cried Professor Spitz. "My time machine is finally ready to test!"

25. "I'm sure of it," groaned Simon. "We're lost."

26. Dear Diary, this may be my last entry.

27. Most villages have an idiot. The village of Corne-on-the-Kobb has hundreds.

28. The old house had boarded-up windows and a door that hung open invitingly.

29. "That's funny," said Matt, "I don't remember downloading this app."

30. Life is strange when you're a bird.

31. Once upon a time, deep underground . . .

32. I had brought an umbrella with me, but that doesn't help so much when it's raining frogs.

33. It all started when I looked inside my satchel and realized that I'd forgotten my gym clothes.

34. Dear Superman . . .

35. Jesse awoke with a strange squealing in his ear.

36. How far out to sea was I? There was certainly no sight of land.

37. I used to love cakes. That is, until yesterday.

38. The floods are coming.

39. The coin was silver, chipped, and older than anything he'd ever seen.

40. The postcard was for me, or so it said. But I didn't recognize the handwriting.

41. Do you believe in dragons?

42. I think it was the day after tomorrow when time started going backward.

43. Midnight, January 1, 1988.

44. "Everyone to their posts. Spades at the ready!" called the mayor.

45. It was the day they lost the boat.

46. Mubbly was a very unusual creature.

47. "Ker-flip," went the large brown envelope as it landed on the hall floor.

48. Aurora looked down at the fang marks on her left hand.

49. The beast was striped with gold and white. Its eyes were flames.

50. I looked at the boy and frowned. "Don't I know you?"

51. As the plane landed, Jack felt a little nervous.

52. The room felt hot. Almost too hot.

53. It was when I took off my shoes that I noticed the roots.

54. The weatherman said it was going to be a sunny day, but outside Susanne saw only snow.

55. Purple. Everything was purple.

56. "I've buried it," she said, "and they'll never find it."

57. The mountain was shrouded with cloud, yet the bloodred summit still poked out from above.

58. "Good morning, Your Majesty," said the well-dressed stranger.

59. In the beginning was a toad.

60. "Just a little off the fringe, please," said Lottie as she sat in the hairdresser's chair.

61. The sun never rose today.

62. When the fire died down, all that remained of the forest was a sea of charred stalks.

63. Why do all my best friends have sticky-out ears?

64. "Come over here!" whispered the bush. "I've got something to tell you."

65. If Tom had any idea what was going on in Sophie's head, he wouldn't have sat next to her that morning.

66. There was once a god who started a primordial soup kitchen.

67. I jumped in headfirst and the freezing darkness enveloped me.

68. The witch stirred her cauldron, a malicious grin on her face.

69. "Darling? This soup is delicious, but don't you think it tastes a little . . . muddy?"

70. Everything I say seems to rhyme.

71. The ice cracked.

72. When the darkness fell, it came quickly and without apology.

73. It had been three weeks since I set foot outside this room.

74. The end.

75. This corridor used to have four doors coming off it. Now there are five.

76. That day, I brought my brother along.

77. "Who's there?" I called, but there was no reply. This was no joke.

78. "Jimmy! Stay away from the edge!"

79. Somewhere in space, a telephone rang.

80. "I'm free!" he cried, as the cell door slammed shut.

81. Do you believe in elves? I don't.

82. Did I ever tell you about the day I learned to fly?

83. "Let go!" I screamed. I would regret that.

84. It wasn't exactly a dog. Dogs don't have all those tubes.

85. The moment she began to sing, the first lightbulb smashed.

86. Tails. Heads. Tails. Heads. Tails. Heads. Tails. Heads.

87. Nobody spotted the sack under Monty's arm when he arrived at the zoo that morning.

88. "Platform five for the 11:36 to Bradley Castle."

89. Tick, tock, tick, tock, tick, tock . . .

90. It looked like a raspberry. It smelled like a raspberry. It sounded, however, like Beyoncé.

91. "So tell me, Adam," she said. "When did you first notice you had no reflection?"

92. The pennies jingled in little Emmy's pocket.

93. I'm down to my final crust of bread.

94. There is a map of Africa on the ceiling above my bed.

95. "Steve?" Mrs. McCauley sung. "It's time for your dance presentation!"

96. There is a thing in the bath. It's green, and slimy, and it wants to know my Wi-Fi password.

97. Anne had lived in her house for thirty-three years. Long enough to know everything about it, right?

98. I found the diamond ring baked inside my morning muffin.

99. "One million green bottles, sitting on the wall," she began.

100. Then, I popped.

Ideas Bank 8:

CATEGORIES

These are for use in **Top Ten of Everything** (page 51), **Pat Clap Click Click** (page 108), **Category Scramble** (page 159), **Letter Links** (page 193), and **A–Z of . . .** (page 214). Each is a category of things, some more literal than others, some wider and easier to fill than others.

Animals	Makes of car
Boys' names	Girls' names
Countries	Landmarks
Musicians	Historical figures
Food and drink	Kitchen items
Colors	Films
Christmas things	Words with four letters
Dog breeds	Brand names
School subjects	TV shows
Hobbies	Sweets
Clothing	Bathroom items
Soccer clubs	Flowers
Villains and monsters	Sports
Towns/cities	Video games
Cartoon characters	Toys and games

Green things	Red things
Black things	White things
Crunchy things	Bouncy things
Light things	Heavy things
Big things	Small things
Messy things	Ugly things
Expensive things	Round things

ACKNOWLEDGMENTS

Writing this book was not a single-player campaign. Wittingly or not, my dozens of tutees and hundreds of pupils have helped refine these games over the years. I owe my pals Charlie, Marianne, Charlotte, and Alice, who eagerly taught me particular games in this book, as well as a lifetime full of colleagues, teachers, and friends who have inspired many more.

Thanks to Eve White, my agent, and to Kate Miles and Lindsay Davies at Headline Home for their amazing editing. Thanks also to Becky Hunter, Caroline Young, Louise Rothwell, Sarah Badhan, and Rob Chilver at Headline.

So much of this book can be blamed on my incredible parents, who know the value of a good game and never made the mistake of telling me to grow up.

Most of all, I want to thank the two women in my life, Olive and Amy, one of whom is a cat and one of whom isn't, but that's not her fault.

INDEX